The Compelling Indwelling

The Compelling Indwelling

By

JAMES H. JAUNCEY

Foreword by

GRADY B. WILSON

MOODY PRESS
CHICAGO

Library of Congress Catalog Card Number: 72-77941

ISBN: 0-8024-1605-5

Printed in the United States of America

To
Martha Miller
whose kindness and encouragement
did much to contribute to the
writing of this book

Contents

Foreword

BILLY GRAHAM has remarked that although he is everywhere finding a decline in interest in institutional religion, the attraction of Jesus Christ Himself shows no signs of losing appeal. Since this appears to be true, the task in this revolutionary generation is to strip away the outworn nonessentials and concentrate on His basic message.

His great mission was to persuade people to so commit themselves in faith to Him and His way of life that God could regenerate them from within, thus transforming their lives and the society to which they belong. The message contained in John 15 is one of His most important and detailed expositions of this truth. It is an exciting portrayal of what God can do if we cooperate.

I think the best way to grasp the magnitude of this message is first to read the exposition through and see the whole majestic panorama, and then to study the exquisite individual scenes in detail. The book has been set out to make this possible. While the sections of the chapters contribute to the total message, each one is complete in itself and may be used as the thought for the day in the private devotional, thus greatly compounding the spiritual impact.

I hope the study inspires you as it does me.

GRADY B. WILSON
Associate Evangelist

Billy Graham Evangelistic Association

1

Transformation from Within

JOHN 15

The Power Within

THE MESSAGE of John 15 is one of the most choice truths that Jesus ever proclaimed because it tells the secret of inner power: the good news that He Himself is going to be within the human spirit, transforming us in spite of ourselves and our weaknesses.

He explains that the Christian way of living is like the vine and its fruit. The only way in which grapes can grow is through the sap of the vine flowing through the branches to work out its God-given purpose of bearing fruit. The branch is completely and utterly dependent on what the vine does for it.

Christ is the vine and we are the branches. Instead of His being merely a teacher telling us what to do, He is going to be within us, generating the kind of power that produces abundant living. Our success is to depend not on our own puny efforts but on the degree of our association with Him.

The fruit is the reproduction in us of the qualities of the personality of Christ: His goodness, His freedom from evil, His awareness of God, His realization of His full human potential, His deep satisfaction and significance in living, His power to be and to do.

He is telling us the exciting news that what He was in His

human life, we too can become, because He wants to live again in and through us.

It has been said that all the teachings of Jesus can be found, at least in fragmentary or germ form, in previous philosophies. Since God always has been speaking to man, this could very well be true. But Jesus alone of all the teachers promised that He would make this way of living feasible by personally transforming the personality from within.

Sad to say, this is the element that is most missed by well-meaning Christians. They see their faith as a philosophy of life, a system of beliefs, a code of ethics, a special program to which they must conform. Because of human frailty, the attempt to achieve all this can become an almost impossible burden on the human spirit.

But Jesus never intended His way to be a burden. He wanted it to be a buoyancy.

He knows that being a Christian in His sense is unnatural to our self-centered hearts, so He proceeds to change them by His Spirit so that His way becomes more and more natural.

This is why Christianity is good news.

Abundant Living

It is easy to see why Jesus felt that this emphasis was so important. The predominant concern of all His teachings was personal living, and this is the key to it. He said once (Jn 10:10) that His purpose in coming was to bring abundant living. His whole outlook was so geared to this end that He gave little attention to anything else.

Great social questions, political controversies, and religious issues were rending the peace of His world, yet He gave them scant attention. He sternly refused to take part in any kind of activism, even though His beloved country was in the grip of a tyrannical occupying power, and social injustice was rampant on every hand. Yet in the long run, His influence has done more to move the conscience of humanity against infringements to human freedom and dignity than anything else in the history of the world.

His idea was to change society by changing men.

Neither did He give any attention to organizing a religious structure. He had no church of His own making, no services, no program, no manuals of operation, no buildings, no officers. His disciples were merely heralds of His message. His bequest when He left was not a constitution for the carrying on of His movement but simply the gift of the Holy Spirit.

It has been said that Jesus did not start a new religion but rather a new philosophy of living. Since then *we* have structured it (either for good or bad), but He didn't. All He wanted to do was to show people how to come into union with God so that He could transform their lives into contentment and useful service.

To capture the genius of His message, we need to recapture this concept. The success of Christianity is not measured by rate of increase in church membership or anything else related to institutionalized religion. It is solely determined by the progress of the kingdom of God in our hearts and through us to others. In the eyes of God, the anguished social conscience of our time concerning race, war, poverty, and human dignity may be the real indicator of the low power of present-day Christianity rather than the decay of formal religion.

Now social action and some amount of religious organization are always necessary, but Jesus would warn us that they can be cheap diversions from those personal issues where basic action is always imperative. The crusade to change society or others is ever more attractive than the mission to transform ourselves. Yet without regenerated man, all the best attempts to reform society are as vain as plastering up a termite-ridden house.

Personal transformation is what God wants first. We have to be prepared to pay that price. If we are, He will do the rest.

Spiritual Pregnancy

This teaching in John 15 about the transforming power of God in the personality is not new in the message of Jesus. It occurs with dramatic impact in His interview with Nicodemus in John 3, the "born again" passage.

It seems quite likely that Nicodemus was an excellent fellow, devoted to God, anxious to learn, and probably dedicated in his service to others. Since these things are the core of Christian living, it might seem that Jesus would have little to add. Instead, He staggers the man by telling him that a complete spiritual rebirth is necessary.

Here Jesus makes it clear that mere reformation misses the mark of what He is aiming for by a million miles. He wants to remake us from within, not just challenge us to mend our ways. He not only wants a certain way of life. He wants to originate and generate it Himself.

The derivation of the Greek word for born again is significant. It originally designated fathered or conceived. This means that true conversion is the impregnation of our human spirit by the Spirit of God, bringing about a new creation, partly human and partly divine. Just as a new human life comes from a fertilized ovum which is part father and part mother, the Christian is similarly a new being.

The physical child is a completely new being from his parents. He comes from them, but he is a separate physical entity and personality. Yet no matter how big he grows, he never can be anything more than what was potential in those genes that his mother and his father gave him. It is one of the amazing facts of life that even the six-foot-four giant on the football field is the product of one tiny, fertilized cell. It is just as astonishing that he might be the child of a petite woman, so frail that the wind could almost blow her away.

The new creature that we are in Christ is almost as separate from our old self as a child is from his mother. At conversion there is a new start. Out of the old self has emerged a spiritual cell which is now a union between God and man. What we can become is in no way limited by what our original mother self was.

What ensues shows a close correspondence with the physical fetal stage of life. Just as the fetus is still surrounded by the mother and remains in that environment until birth, so also the spiritual fetus is enclosed in the old personality. People looking at us see the same person. A photograph before and after conversion would show no physical difference. Yet a miracle of spiritual life has started within which will develop its own life and will subsequently emerge to live an independent existence. This will happen at death. Until then, I am a growing, divine-human creation on its way to full maturity.

The analogy can be continued. The newborn child has characteristics of his father because he has his father's blood in his veins. In the same way, the newborn spiritual child should show the spiritual characteristics of the heavenly Father because of the spiritual genes which he has inherited.

Just as a child does not have to try to be like his father, so we should not have to try to hard to reproduce the image of God. It should be a natural process.

Much evangelism misses the depth of this teaching. Conversion is often treated very superficially as some kind of bargain made with God or acquiescence with a set of beliefs or acceptance of what is referred to as "the plan of salvation."

Instead, conversion implies a total change of being. The purely human is replaced by the divine-human entity. Christian living is the outworking of the indwelling Christ. Athanasius referred to it as the "deification of the personality," the progressive taking over of the human by the divine.

Total Committal

The word *salvation* has now become a technical term in theology, traditionally referring to eligibility to enter heaven. But in the New Testament it simply means deliverance and usually refers to deliverance from the guilt and power of sin, which then makes us citizens of heaven.

Conversion means the start of that process. It removes the guilt of sin and makes the person a child of God. It introduces the Spirit of God into the personality, who then proceeds to act like a spiritual antibiotic to attack the germs of evil. This takes time. It is quite unrealistic to imagine that all the power and presence of sin will disappear at conversion. It is the beginning of the process.

Quite a lot of theological speculation has gone on as to what are the conditions of salvation. By this is meant those requirements in the seeker which must be fulfilled before God will act, and if not carried out will prevent His Spirit entering the heart.

Strange to say, the Bible does not set up any iron-clad rules. Some are called simply to believe, some to repent, some to follow, some to be baptized, one to sell all his goods, and others with various combinations of these. But if we look closely, we find that there is a common denominator in every case, and that is total committal. God only acts when the whole personality is unreservedly given over to Him.

To most of us, there is a barrier to this surrender which is unique to us personally. To the rich young ruler it was greed, so that had to be singled out. God puts His finger on the critical point of issue, and this may not be the same with everyone.

Luther built his Reformation on faith alone as the sole, sufficient condition for salvation. But he did not mean mere intellectual belief. He considered faith to be unrealistic unless it involved the willingness to obey all the commands of Christ and follow Him at all cost.

It is noteworthy that the New Testament does not ask us merely to believe Christ. It demands belief *in* Christ. There is a world of difference. Belief is easy. "The devils also believe and tremble" (James 2:19). But *believing in* means trusting in. It means having such confidence in Christ and His way of life that we commit ourselves unreservedly to Him. That kind of faith is real tough.

The Christian faith was never intended to be easy. It is the way of the cross. To gain that faith we have to give up ourselves. But once we do, the prize is great: Christ gives Himself to us.

Grace Versus Works

All this ties in with the great obsession of the apostle Paul.

Almost to the point of tediousness, he insists that salvation is not of works but is the free gift of the grace of God. We don't use that word *grace* much anymore in this sense. It means kindness, generosity, benevolence.

By *works* Paul means anything we might do to earn our salvation. He insists that there is no way to accumulate merit as a kind of spiritual credit balance. Good deeds, religious observances, personal reformation, orthodoxy in belief—they don't count for a thing in this respect. It is only when we give up trying to be worthy of Jesus and take Him as a gift that we can find eternal life .

This teaching is well known in evangelical circles. Indeed, it is at the heart of the gospel message. But Paul is referring to much more than conversion here. He is meaning the whole long process of salvation, the lifelong emancipation from sin. This is also a gift from God.

Many Christians abandon grace at conversion and assume that after that they have to rely on works. They think that they have to struggle by sheer will power to eliminate evil. Paul says, "No! God wants to do the eliminating. All we need to do is to let Him."

His most graphic illustration comes in Romans 7. After agonizingly describing the failure of the human will to conquer inner evil ("For the good that I would I do not: but the evil which I would not that I do," v. 19), he cries out in anguish, "O wretched man that I am! Who shall deliver me from the body of this death?" (v. 24).

It is thought that he is here using the rather horrible analogy of the Roman practice of chaining a murderer to his victim and letting him die in the arms of the corpse. Paul felt his enslavement to evil was just that terrible.

But he answers his own question. "I thank God through Jesus Christ our Lord." Christ is the deliverer! Since the enslavement is within, He frees from within by His own Spirit.

The indwelling Christ is a frequent theme with Paul and we can see why. It is his secret of victory and power. The victory that he could not win, even with that amazing will of his, was won by Christ without effort. It did not come in a moment, and he never achieved perfection; but nevertheless, the time came when he was no longer a slave.

This is exactly what Jesus is teaching in the parable of the vine and the branches.

It is like the difference between rowing a heavy boat or using the inboard engine. If the tide is against you, you strain uselessly at the oars, but once you kick that engine into action, you can sit back and enjoy yourself while the boat effortlessly rides the waves.

The Fruit of the Spirit

One of the clearest examples of how well the teachings of Paul reflect the very heart of what Jesus is saying is in Galatians 5:22-23: "But the fruit of the Spirit is love, joy, peace, longsuffering, gentleness, goodness, faith, meekness, temperance." Here the analogy is the same as in John 15. The Christian virtues are the fruit of the Spirit. They do not come about artificially as the products of the human will. They are the fruits which come naturally from the source of life within. You don't have to manufacture them or, even worse, fake them. You let God bring them into being, just as the sap of the tree engenders its fruit.

There is some question among commentators whether "Spirit" in this passage should be spelled with a capital *s* or not. The original Greek text of the New Testament was all in capitals, every letter, so we can't tell from that. The issue is that if a capital is intended, the Holy Spirit is referred to, but if a small letter, the human spirit.

Paul's obsession with the idea of Christ the Holy Spirit indwelling us makes it almost certain, in my mind, that this is his meaning here, but actually it doesn't matter. The essential reference is to the spiritual, inner source. As seen earlier in Christ's teaching on conversion, that inner spirit is both human and divine, a new creation, a God-impregnated spirit. Therefore, whether we use *Spirit* or *spirit* merely reflects if we are viewing the matter from a divine or human point of view. The reality is the same.

Now Paul has nothing against human action. As we have seen in his feeling against works, he objects to mere human initiative.

Virtues that come from self-effort are both artificial and transient. They are as artificial as flowers tied on shrubs and about as permanent. For an evening's garden party this practice might have value, but it is certainly not regular gardening procedure.

Producing and maintaining Christian virtues on our own is a heartbreaking procedure. It is so hard and so against the grain that it makes life burdensome. Christianity was never intended to be that.

But Paul would have another objection to ersatz virtues. They leave God out and make Christian living essentially nonreligious. The atheist can do just as well at will-power goodness as the Christian. Paul cannot conceive of a God who stands back and tells people to do things. The God of the Christian is an active God who is in there working to bring about what He demands.

The Christian who is abiding in Christ can stop worrying whether he will make the grade in developing personal goodness. Instead he can sense the divine Spirit within and have the faith to know that the fruit is on its way.

Proof That God Exists

This teaching that Christ is active in the life, transforming it from within, pays an important and perhaps unexpected dividend. It proves experimentally to the one who experiences it that God does exist.

Since nowadays the only proof that most people will accept is experiential rather than theoretical, this is of the greatest importance. The older theoretical proofs were of the *must* variety. God *must* exist; otherwise, how do you explain the origin of the universe or design in nature or the source of goodness?

Such thinking does carry some weight, but it is not very convincing to modern man. He needs something more tangible.

Probably some of our skepticism about theoretical proofs is the result of experience. We were told the moon *must* have a deposit of dust on it that might drown an astronaut, that automation *must* produce unemployment, that UFO's mean that we *must* be receiving visits from the outer space, and so on. Yet experience has shown that these conclusions were far from valid. Even the greatest thinkers err. Newton inferred that man could not travel beyond 60 miles per hour. Edison concluded that the electronic effect could not have much practical usefulness. Facts so often belie theory.

When Jesus was asked about what evidence there was that He came from God, He didn't theorize. He pointed to what was happening. It is the action of God that makes us aware that He is there.

When we see grapes on a vine, it is not a great strain on our credulity to believe that they are there because of an inner source of life. When we experience transforming power in our lives that accomplishes what we cannot ourselves, we know that God is there. Actually, it is more than merely deducing that He is there. We sense His presence. In a strange mysterious way, we know.

Fortunately, this is not transferable. It is true that an onlooker can watch my life and conclude that a higher power must be at work, but he cannot look into my soul and see that power. The best that can happen is that he can be so convinced that he will take the jump of faith to experience it for himself. In the long run, he does have to find it for himself.

The Christian's own certainty is personal. It comes from his own confrontation with God as God works within him.

This is undoubtedly the great task for evangelism today. Christ needs to be proclaimed, not merely theoretically as in preaching or theology, but in living testimony. It is noteworthy that the New Testament does not merely demand that we witness. That is too easy and too unconvincing. It asks that we *be* witnesses, which is much more difficult but infinitely more convincing.

We live in a world which is no longer willing to take things on trust. If we say there is a God, it wants to see the results of His action. That has to be far more than what could come from self-effort.

Jesus makes it clear in John 15 that God is prepared to take up this challenge. He wants to show Himself among men, not by bizarre or magical stunts but by solid power in transforming human lives. Whether He does so or not depends on us. He won't burglarize the soul even for the most desirable ends. We have to allow Him. In Jesus' own words, "abide in Me."

He is offering us power to become. Let us see how He works this message out in detail.

2

God the Gardener

VERSES 1-2

The Continuing Care

THE TRUTH that conversion is a divine implantation in the life might lead us to assume that the action stops there, as with a man who plants a garden and then leaves it, hoping for the best. This absentee-landlord theory has always been somewhat popular. It is technically called deism.

The deist thinks that this is what God has done to the world as a whole. He started the whole thing off and now passively sits back to watch the unfolding of the natural laws that He placed in it.

This is certainly not the God of the Bible. God is ever the husbandman, the vinetender, the gardener. "I am the true vine, and my Father is the husbandman" (v. 1). Jesus makes it clear that what God starts in conversion requires both divine and human continuing action.

God takes into account that there is more to be concerned with than the embryonic spiritual life. There is evil as well as good, and the evil is always encroaching on the good. There are weeds that could choke out the life of the new seedling. There are parasites that could devour it. There are natural elements—wind, rain, cold, and heat— that could destroy it. The care of the gardener is always needed.

The spiritual life of the Christian is under continuous attack. It is faced with enemies on every hand. The most persistent and subtle of these are within us, our own selfishness and folly, but this is only a fraction of the problem. The inner life may be damaged by the wickedness and even the kindness of others. It may be hurt by the ups and downs of circumstances. The spiritual plant is like a garden in the jungle. Without the gardener it could not survive for long.

Some of these dangers are described by Jesus in another analogy, the parable of the sower (Mt 13:3-23). There is the action of the "wicked one" who snatches the seed when the Word is not understood. There is the problem of the stony heart where the Word cannot go deep enough, and the experience is too superficial. There is the threat of the "thorns," the cares and riches of this world. In this parable the Lord is primarily referring to our responsibility to the new life, but He does not leave it to us. He is there with us all the time, eager that it may achieve full growth and fruitfulness.

Many earnest people, when faced with the challenge to commit their lives to Christ, hesitate, appalled by the thought of their own weaknesses or by the magnitude of what is against them. They needn't feel like that, because God is with us, accomplishing His purposes.

The life of Jesus is a constant reminder of this. One of His earliest titles was *Immanuel* which means "God with us." In Christ, God was present in person in our world, to suffer and toil with us. This will always be true in our lives because of the indwelling Christ. The gardener is there. All we need to do is to cooperate with Him.

Partnership in Care

Many people think of God's sovereignty in such a fantastic way that they stifle their own initiative. They think of God as a kind of oriental monarch who has everything so cut and dried that his subjects can do nothing about it. This is an insult to human dignity. Man is made in the image of God and determines his own destiny. God woos but does not force.

Not only does He not determine human action, but He also does not substitute Himself for our responsible action.

With some earnest but inexperienced people there sometimes occurs an unfortunate pietism: "leave it to the Lord." I've seen Bible college students get deeply into debt because of this notion, expecting checks to drop like manna from heaven.

One student almost drifted into disastrous circumstances because of this error. He felt that working to pay his way was not having faith. He had been inspired to this belief by a missionary's message of how God had worked miracles for him in the Far East. Ultimately, he had to accept a job. It was as a janitor's assistant. To his surprise, he found that the janitor was that same missionary, who was now working his way through graduate school!

It is worth noting that when Paul needed money for the needy Christians in Jerusalem, he didn't just "leave it to the Lord." He made imperative demands on the Christians abroad to pitch in and help. Paul assumed that God usually worked in and through human channels, not apart from them.

Being surrendered to the Lord does not mean that we become zombies or robots. If God had wanted, He could have made us as machines in the first place, programmed to do His will. What He wants is our cooperation, our partnership in the divine action.

This is not drifting back into a doctrine of works. The difference is something like this: Suppose we have a big rock to be shifted. We could push at it with our puny strength. That would be works. Or we could drive a bulldozer and let it move the rock. That would be grace. However, the dozer won't do it on its own. We still have to drive it.

This is particularly true of divine guidance. Except in most unusual circumstances, this is not something apart from the mind. We still have to think, but the indwelling Christ who permeates the whole personality helps us in our reasoning and guides us through it.

Coming back to the garden analogy, this message means that the head gardener does not do all the work. Neither does

He abandon us to our inexperience to tend it ourselves. Patiently and kindly He teaches us the art, working with us and through us, so that His plan is fulfilled, yet the accomplishment has been equally ours.

The Sterile Ones

There is a certain ruthlessness about the task of a gardener. He has to be busy with the knife. It seems a shame that so much has to be cut away; but if the garden is to produce fruit, it is the only way.

Jesus says God has that function, too. "Every branch in me that beareth not fruit he taketh away" (v. 2). This is often interpreted as a kind of punishment for not bearing fruit, but this would be reversing what Christ is teaching. His emphasis is that fruit bearing is a direct and necessary result of union with Himself. It therefore follows that if no fruit is forthcoming, then He cannot be in the heart in the first place.

In other words, He is talking about pseudoconversions, people who go through the religious formalities, but with whom there is no real committal to Christ and therefore no regeneration.

There is an allusion to this difference in the parable of the tares (Mt 13:24-30). These weeds look like wheat and are in there with the wheat, but they are not the wheat. Ultimately, only God can do the sorting out.

The same kind of thing is referred to in Matthew 7:21-23 where Jesus says some call Him Lord but He never knew them. There can be no doubt that Jesus draws a sharp distinction between the genuine and the false. With Him it is not a matter of degrees of ethical behavior. It is whether His life is within or not. Fruit is the evidence of the inner life. "Wherefore by their fruits ye shall know them" (Mt 7:20).

The taking away of the fruitless branches is to occur at the judgment day and is the right of God alone. Nothing could be more improper than for us to go around judging people's genuineness by superficially appraising their lives.

This relationship between fruit bearing and His spiritual impregnation can be unnecessarily disturbing. None of us has the fruit we ought to have. Does this mean that we should doubt our union with God?

This all depends on whether the problem is sterility or a mere temporary trouble. A sterile branch is never going to bear fruit, but a fruitless branch may not be sterile by any means. It may mean that the season for fruit has not yet come, or perhaps that it has some curable problem that is causing trouble.

Spiritual maturation takes time. God has to build up the processes within us before they result in fruit. Also, as we shall see, the degree of fruit bearing depends on how well we are abiding in Him, and maybe this is still a problem with us.

How can we be sure that we do have God within us, if the fruits of the Spirit are not very evident? Well, it doesn't help to go back in our minds and hold a postmortem on our conversion. It isn't necessary anyway, because we can commit or recommit ourselves to God anytime. If we are constantly doing this (and we should be), we are always in the state where He can enter the life.

God does not want us to have a spirit of fear or of insecurity about our acceptance with God. We can be sure of this, that no soul that comes to Him in sincere and unreserved committal will ever be turned away.

The Knife in His Hand

Probably nothing about gardening makes the inexperienced gardener more nervous than pruning. He knows that if he prunes too severely he may kill the tree, and yet if he does not cut back far enough, he will seriously limit the fruit produced. It takes skill and experience to be good at pruning.

Jesus says in verse 2 that God as gardener is the pruner to those lives which have started to bear fruit, so that they may be even more productive. Since pruning involves hurt, we cannot view this activity with much anticipation no matter how necessary it may be. But we can be very glad that the pruning is in the hands of an all-knowing and all-loving God.

Actually, this pruning was necessary even for Christ, for

the epistle to the Hebrews says that God has made the captain of our salvation perfect through suffering (Heb 2:10). At first sight, the idea of adding to His perfection seems to be sheer nonsense, but we have to remember that perfection is a relative term. You may know about suffering perfectly well intellectually, but you know it in quite a different sense emotionally when you go through it yourself. When you go through the harrowing experience of bereavement for the first time, you become only too well aware of this difference. But from His suffering came the greatest fruit of all, our salvation, and it could not have come in any other way.

The presence of suffering in our world is one of the unexplainable things about creation. It seems as useless to probe it as to ask why a centipede has a hundred legs. It is better to take it as an unalterable fact and do what God does—use it. The Bible is insistent that no matter the source of evil—wickedness, accident, ourselves, circumstances—God never lets it run wild over the Christian. It is always directed towards a greater good if we cooperate with Him. "For our light affliction, which is but for a moment, worketh for us a far more exceeding and eternal weight of glory" (2 Co 4:17).

Quite often the pruning of suffering is a necessary means of accomplishing God's purposes for us. The story of Joseph in Genesis is a good illustration. He went through a chain of disasters: sold as a slave, falsely imprisoned, forgotten by the butler he befriended, yet unknown to him, each one of these was a stepping stone to God's ultimate goal for him, the prime ministership of Egypt. We need to remember that being besieged by unhappy events, far from implying that God has abandoned us, means that He is guiding us towards even greater fulfillment. As the writer to the Hebrews puts it: "For whom the Lord loveth he chasteneth" (Heb 12:6).

God's pruning is never too severe, neither for what He has in mind nor for what we can bear. His wisdom prevents the first possibility, and His love excludes the second. He knows our limits so well that He tenderly protects us from the overpowering evil that would break us. "God . . . will not suffer you to be tempted above that ye are able; but will with the temptation also make a way to escape, that ye may be able to bear it" (1 Co 10:13).

The idea of grace in this respect is very encouraging. Paul refers to this in 2 Corinthians 12:9 in connection with his "thorn in the flesh." It means that He not only limits the evil, but He also gives us extra strength and inspiration to endure the trial. In fact, He is there with us in the ordeal.

Death itself is part of the pruning. It cuts away the limitations of the physical body so that the infinite fruitfulness of eternity may become possible. To use another analogy, the caterpillar must go through the apparent death in the cocoon to emerge as the butterfly free to express itself as was never possible before the metamorphosis.

No, we need not fear the knife in the hand of the gardener.

Only as He Directs

Pruning often means cutting off shoots that are growing in the wrong direction. The gardener can see that if the branch grows that way it will interfere with other branches or spread into places which will limit its fruitfulness. Sometimes he fears that it will become unsightly.

God often has to prune us the same way. He sees the end from the beginning and knows where every path will lead, but we don't. We are desperately in need of His guidance. There is no danger to our freedom of initiative in this, anymore than the navigator who steers the ship away from the rocks is doing a disservice to the ship.

Even spiritual giants like Paul had to be subject to this kind of divine action. On his second missionary journey he figured he would go to the Ephesus area, but God had other ideas (Ac 16:6). As it turned out, he was destined to bring the gospel to Europe instead.

God never makes any mistakes about these detours, although it may be hard to believe this at the time.

I must confess that at one time, my being required to work for years at a time as a scientist did not make sense. I had nothing against science. In fact, I loved the work. But I felt that preaching the gospel was so much more urgent and necessary. Surely God must know that this is where I ought to be. Yet, in the long run, the experience and prestige of being a scientist has made my proclamation of the Word infinitely more fruitful.

The timing of a project can be vitally important. What could dismally fail now can easily be a stunning success later. Quite often we do not know enough to detect this, but God does, and to save us unnecessary humiliation or to safeguard His kingdom, He stops us.

It helps to remember this when we are frustrated by barriers to cherished projects: an illness disables us for months on end, an unexpected heavy expense prevents us from going to college or graduate school, trouble to a loved one forces us to step aside for a while to help them, an economic recession lays us off from a needed job, a war takes off years from our life, a mistake forces months of backtracking. God's hand is always at the helm.

There is no need to be apprehensive about guidance. On the whole, since He is in our hearts and minds, we are being guided by God; and we should assume this unless He lets us know otherwise.

God has a plan for every life which, if followed, guarantees the greatest fulfillment. As we have seen, there is no determinism in this. We are not forced to do anything. All He wants is that we should take advantage of His wisdom. Mostly He will do this through our God-impregnated thinking, but occasionally He will need to stop us for our own good. He won't do this unless He knows that this is what we really want. He would rather let us suffer failure than violate the freedom He has given us.

When we see Him about to cut off a cherished shoot, let us not take the knife out of His hands. After all, He knows.

Continuing Fruitfulness

Jesus says that the work of the gardener is to bring about

greater fruitfulness (v. 2). This underlines the *progressive* nature of the fulfillment which comes from the power of the indwelling Christ.

There could hardly be any greater disillusionment than that which would come from assuming an instantaneous transformation at conversion. It is true there are wonderful stories told of really bad people whose chains of sin have been miraculously snapped in a moment of time. God certainly can do this, but He seldom does. The reason why these accounts are so striking is because they are so rare.

We can generally expect God to act gradually. He is perfectly capable of dropping manna from heaven, but mostly He feeds us by a long process that starts with a seed planted in the ground and ends months later in a bakery. He could produce men as ready-made, mature beings. Instead they have to develop for a quarter of a century from a tiny fertilized ovum.

The imagery of spiritual conception in John, chapter 3, referred to earlier is the divine counterpart of what happens on the human scale. The God-conceived new life within still has a long way to go to reach maturity. Therefore for a new convert to say "I don't feel any different" is as meaningless as a newly expectant mother to say the same the morning after impregnation. Not even a doctor can tell that soon.

Spiritual growth can be as unnoticeable as natural growth. Have you ever seen a child angry and frustrated because the seeds he planted the night before haven't come up?

We don't need to worry about growth. All we need to do is to let it happen. Instead of being discouraged about the problems still in the life, we should turn our attention to the silent spiritual antibiotic that is going to destroy them, given time.

Neither is spiritual growth a steady though slow increase. It is more like an incoming tide with its advancing and receding waves. It is foolish to get dispirited about the recessions as it is to get complacent about the advances. Indeed, there will be plateaus where nothing seems to happen at all.

These plateaus occur in some learning processes too, such as with shorthand. A student may increase her proficiency steadily to 40 words per minute and then get stuck there for quite a while until a sudden spurt takes her to a higher level. Then there is another plateau, and so on. It is all very discouraging until she learns that something is happening in these plateaus. They are the unconscious mind's breathing space to build up the resources necessary for the next advance. Spiritual growth is exactly the same.

It is worth noting that Jesus did not promise His disciples to become fishers of men right away. He said, "I will make you to *become* fishers of men" (Mk 1:17, italics added).

It is wonderful to know that the fulfillment and achievement that Jesus calls bearing fruit is dynamic, not static, for it means that we can never reach our limit. The more we achieve, the more we can achieve because the Gardener is bent on accomplishing just that. "Eye hath not seen, nor ear heard, neither have entered into the heart of man, the things which God hath prepared for them that love him" (1 Co 2:9).

3

The Cleansing Word

VERSE 3

Cleansing in Depth

The analogy of the vine and the branches changes slightly in verse 3, but the theme has not altered. What Christ is seeking to bring about is the transformation of the personality through His presence within. This can be considered as fruit bearing generated by His life or as deliverance from the evil in the soul by His inner power, so that fulfillment can come once the barriers are removed. This amounts to cleansing in depth.

It is worthwhile noticing that the term *sin* is used in several ways in the Bible. It may mean sin as guilt. It may refer to sin as the practice of doing wrong. It may imply sin as a principle or power that enslaves us. Cleansing is needed in each of these senses.

Sin as guilt is one of the big theological problems to which Paul addresses himself in the early chapters of the epistle to the Romans. Here he means it in a legal sense, not the psychological, as when a person *feels* guilty. Man has broken God's law and is under His indictment. Christ saves us from penalty by His death. The pardon comes as a free gift from God once we commit ourselves to Him by faith. This objective guilt is removed at conversion.

Sad to say, it is possible to feel guilty even after the legal guilt has been removed. This is totally unnecessary torture. It can easily be dissipated by simply taking God at His word: "The blood of Jesus Christ his Son cleanseth us from all sin" (1 Jn 1:7). This simple realization can bring tremendous relief and peace.

Actually, guilt is the easiest sin problem to deal with. The practice and power of sin is something else because it is a lifelong problem. Cleansing from guilt occurs in a moment, but eradication of actual sin is continuous throughout life. No matter how much we accomplish, there is always more. "If we say that we have no sin, we deceive ourselves, and the truth is not in us" (1 Jn 1:8).

Sin here means far more than really bad deeds such as crimes. It means anything that is rebellious to God, everything that hurts others, and whatever hinders the greatest fulfillment that we are capable of.

Jesus explained in the Sermon on the Mount that sins are not isolated acts. They spring from an inner principle of evil. Anger brings murder, lust produces adultery, and so on. Therefore cleansing from the mere acts of sin is as useless as attempting to rub off measles spots. To accomplish anything significant, you have to get at the inner disease.

We already have seen that the life of Christ within does exactly that by acting as a spiritual antibiotic. But in this verse Jesus brings in another slant on how this is accomplished. It is through the Word.

The Radioactive Word

The term *the word* in the New Testament has a different meaning from what it does in English, such as when we speak of words in a sentence. It is the translation of the Greek word *logos* which has no English equivalent. The nearest we get to it is in combination words such as *biology* and *psychology,* where the *-logy* ending comes from *logos* and means something like "knowledge about."

Logos was a popular term with Alexandrian philosophers who thought of it as knowledge that comes from divine action. They considered God as the source of mental energy just as we think of the sun as the source of physical energy. Waves go out from God and impinge on the mind of man and then emerge as knowledge. As many of them saw it, scholars do not create knowledge, they merely reflect it. This stream of thought from God is Logos, the Word.

Possibly the nearest we could come to it is *message*. It has deep theological and practical significance. It implies that God is constantly seeking to make Himself known to us. But it is not so much intellectual knowledge which He wishes to impart but life knowledge. Rather than tell us what He is like, He wants to show us Himself by reproducing His image within us.

Therefore, if we expect God to solve the problem of the Trinity for us or explain what heaven is like, we are going to be disappointed. He is more likely to point out how wrong it is to be irritable and sour, or how we can hold up under stress. He seldom passes out truths to individual persons which are valid for all people at all times. Instead, He often tailors His message to meet my personal needs here and now.

This process of God speaking to the heart is continual, something like a spiritual radioactive bombardment. Its action on the evil in the life is similar to that of an isotope zeroed in on cancerous tissue. It destroys it and cleanses the organism. This is what Jesus means when He speaks of the cleansing Word.

The impact of the Word on the personality cannot be expected to be pleasant always. We cannot come under that bombardment without being acutely conscious of the wrong within and how it robs the kingdom of God, hurts others, and eats away at their fulfillment as well as our own. The Word is sharper than a two-edged sword and the surrendered Christian must be prepared to feel that edge. This takes courage, but beyond the hurt is greater fulfillment than we have ever known.

The Living Word

The most sensational use of the Word in the New Testament occurs in the first few verses of the gospel of John. He says

Jesus is the Word, and in so doing raises the idea to a staggering height of meaning undreamed of by the Greeks.

They could conceive of God transmitting His message to mankind in words, but here John claims that He did it in person. In science fiction we sometimes read of a man being changed into energy by a machine, and as energy transmitted like radio waves to a distant point where another machine changes him back into a human body. John's conception is not unlike this. Of course, he knows God is spirit not matter, because he himself quotes Jesus as saying this (Jn 4:24), so there is no suggestion of bodily transfer. But he does say that the Word was made flesh and dwelt amongst us (Jn 1:14). In some mysterious way, in Jesus the Word becomes a living person.

Now the purpose of the Word is to reflect or reveal God. This means that Jesus is the revelation of God, the image of God. Although the body of Jesus is not God, since God is spirit and does not have a fleshly body, His person is God. Jesus Himself makes this very clear when Philip asked to see the Father. "Have I been so long time with you, and yet hast thou not known me, Philip?" he asked. "He that hath seen me hath seen the Father" (Jn 14:9).

Too much time has been wasted by people trying to guess how this could be. That is academic. The vital thing is what it means for us. The main significance is that since God is present in Christ, we can stop speculating about God and we do not need to be confined in our knowledge of Him to the inadequacy of words. We see God in a life.

This was a great discovery to me as a boy. The religious background of my youth was repressive with strong Old Testament overtones. No matter how I tried, I found it too difficult to like God although I knew I should. He was too much of the ogre. But when I learned that God was like Jesus, the whole picture changed. It was easy to love a God like that person.

The marvellous thing about Jesus is that in Him we can sense what God is like without attempting to define Him. In fact, when we try to put what we see in Christ into words, we slip into confusing inadequacy. He is too big and too wonderful for that. He is the living Word.

This is the Word that we are told in John 15 is within us. His very presence within the soul cleanses and ennobles. In the flesh, He didn't have to tell extortioner Zacchaeus to make restitution. Just being there was enough to purge that wayward heart (Lk 19:1-8).

It is even better with us. We are not up in a sycamore tree looking down at Him on a dusty Palestinian road. He is much closer than that. He is within our hearts. He had to leave Zacchaeus, but He never has to leave us because He abides with us.

The Written Word

Usually when we refer to the Word of God now we mean the Bible but, curiously enough, this does not seem to be the New Testament practice. There the writers usually call the Bible the Scriptures. But they leave no doubt that the Bible is indeed the Word of God. They believed that it was God's message when it was written, and that God is still speaking through it to the heart.

Much needless theological dispute has been wasted on the question of how God inspired the writers in the first place. We simply do not know. It is evident that He worked through their minds and hearts because their writings retain their individual characteristics. There was no infringement on their freedom or dignity, but nevertheless He did get His message through.

We must not think of the Bible as some kind of textbook. It is rather the divinely inspired record of God's dealings with men. It is not a fixed deposit of truth to be put away in the archives. It is meant to be the vehicle of God's message to men at all times.

This is what inspiration really means, not only that God inspired it in the first place, but that He inspires it now. For practical purposes, it is far more important that God should inspire the readers than he should the writers, because they are the real ones that God has in mind. God the Holy Spirit is resident in the Scriptures, eager to take them and apply them to any needy heart.

Therefore, if we go to the Bible merely for information, we will miss its main purpose. We should read it so that God can speak to us about our lives.

Merely absorbing the print will not accomplish this purpose. We have to consciously open our hearts to God's voice. It works this way: Suppose I read a Bible story. I must ask myself what God is teaching me through this story. What sins did this man commit that I must avoid? What virtues did he attain that I must emulate? What help and insight did he gain with his problems that can help me in mine? This way the Bible becomes sharply relevant to my life here and now.

What happens is that the Bible sheds light on the inner reaches of the personality, revealing what is still wrong.

The Old Testament itself comes very close to the words of Jesus in describing its action on the human spirit. "Wherewithal shall a young man cleanse his way? by taking heed thereto according to thy word" (Ps 119:9).

This emphasizes the truth that the mere message of the Word does not cleanse. It merely shows where the cleansing must take place. The cleansing comes when we respond.

The Spoken Word

In the last section it was stated that the New Testament writers use the term Word of God in a different sense than we do for we mean the Bible. Instead they use it to mean the message of God that comes in preaching, especially the gospel proclamation. We see it in expressions such as "they . . . went every where preaching the word" (Ac 8:4). A checkup on New Testament sermons shows that although they used their Bible (the Old Testament), they certainly did not preach it. They preached Christ, His death and resurrection, and the need for sinners to commit themselves to Him in faith.

They did not mean that there was anything infallible about their sermons—far from it. But they did have an intense conviction that God was so vitally interested in reaching men that He spoke through them. It was this *speaking through* that constituted the Word rather than the words they used.

In view of what the Bible teaches about the part of the Holy Spirit in conversion, this has great significance. Conversion does involve a human committal, but it is essentially a divine act. Mere persuasion is completely inadequate. Indeed, it may bring about a sad imitation of conversion. Nothing happens regardless of the degree of reformation unless God enters the soul.

Of course, only a small part of preaching is directed towards getting converts. Most preaching has as its goal the development of Christian living. But, as we have seen, there also is the work of the Holy Spirit. It adds up to the fact that all preaching must be a channel for God's voice to reach the soul.

Without this ingredient of the Word, all preaching seems foolish, as Paul readily admits (1 Co 1:18). Probably 99 percent of all sermons is forgotten by 99 percent of the people almost as soon as the delivery is over. Probably within a week the minister has forgotten it himself. This seems to be a foolish waste, but it never is if God is in the message, because the impact He makes on the heart lives on. Madame Curie boiled up tons of pitchblende to get that microscopic particle of radium, but it was infinitely worth it.

Because of the Word of God in preaching, He can reach people in spite of human errors. An illiterate evangelist preached a sermon on "the heathen being as those who scratch a board," in the belief that this was what his text said when read to him. Actually it referred to "the heathen being scattered abroad." Graphically he described the painful splinters in the nails that would result from the rejection of Christ. In spite of his mistake, several people were converted!

Protestant congregations are rather prone to look on preaching as a means of entertainment. This doctrine of the Word can change all that. Instead we should listen to every sermon expectantly, knowing that God is eager to speak to us through it.

The Word of God in preaching does cleanse. As human beings, ministers are living in the midst of human weakness and they know! God uses this experiential insight to pinpoint the evil spots in the soul. Once again, of course, the actual work depends on our response, for there is nothing so deadly as inspiration without action.

The Intimate Word

I am aware that this discussion on verse 3 has ranged rather far afield and may have gone considerably further than Jesus intended in this immediate context. However, it has not been irrelevant or speculative. The concept of the Word in the New Testament is one cohesive idea, and when we touch on one aspect we assume the whole; and that single aspect is best understood in terms of the whole picture.

But here Jesus seems to limit the reference not only to the spoken Word but, in particular, to that which He has said to them. "Now ye are clean through the word which I have spoken unto you." It could be, of course, that He is talking about the cleansing power of His message in general and this would certainly be possible in view of what has been said above. But such a meaning would be somewhat out of context here. It has to tie in with what He is saying about the vine and the branches.

Perhaps we can paraphrase it like this: "Now this truth that I have just spoken to you, of the Vine and the Branches, is the secret of the cleansing of your personalities. God's Word is always cleansing, but this Word from Him through Me is particularly important."

Now Jesus does not mean that there is anything magical about the vine and branches statement such that it automatically cleanses on merely hearing it. That would violate His principles of human responsibility. He makes this clear in His warning at the end of the Sermon on the Mount. "Therefore whosoever heareth these sayings of mine, *and doeth them,* I will liken him unto a wise man, which built his house upon a rock: . . . And every one that heareth these sayings of mine, and *doeth them not,* shall be likened unto a foolish man, which built his house upon the sand" (Mt 7:24, 26, italics added).

It isn't His actual words that cleanse, but the truth that they express. The message of the vine and the branches is that the living Word is within. It is not a spiritual action like cosmic rays where the impact comes from a distance, or even like a radioactive source in a machine close by focused on the soul. The spiritual isotope is within the life. God has operated on the body spiritual and inserted the Word within us.

The difference between this aspect of the Word and the others is intimacy. God is giving us personalized treatment. We are not in a mob being showered with spiritual radioactivity in the hope that some will reach us. God is directing our treatment in terms of our personal needs and from within.

Every human being likes to feel that he is something special. This is not mere pride. It is the way God made us. The Christian faith meets this need. There is no mass production with God. In a very tender way Jesus expressed this personal concern in the words, "But even the very hairs of your head are all numbered" (Lk 12:7).

The teaching about the indwelling Christ presents to us this unique relationship. We are each a union between the self and God, and no other relationship can be quite like it.

What Jesus is saying in this verse is that God wants to cleanse the personality of its evil elements, and that He is going to do this—with our cooperation—by the presence of the living Word within.

4

The Abiding

VERSE 4

THE HUMAN RESPONSE

THE MESSAGE of Jesus about the vine and the branches starts with heavy emphasis on the part that God plays. When we commit ourselves to Him, we become a branch on the true vine, and His life sustains us by flowing through us. It is this life which produces the fruit. At first sight, it would appear that all we have to do is to passively let it happen. But as the teaching progresses, we detect an increasing emphasis on the human side until it becomes clear that nothing much can happen without continuous human response.

This comes out rather abruptly in verse 4. Jesus says, "Abide in me and I in you." The word *abide* is now almost obsolete in ordinary language. The nearest we get to it is when we speak of a person having or not having a fixed "abode," and even that word is beginning to sound odd. But this is the meaning of the term, a place to stay and live. Jesus is saying that we must live with Him if we want to bear the fruits of the Spirit.

Here Jesus is changing the analogy a little so that He can emphasize the human responsibility. With the vine and branches illustration this is a little difficult. When the branch has been produced by the vine, you don't have to tell it to stay there. This is true only if its *existence* is thought of. But

Jesus has more in mind than this. It is *fruitfulness* that He is after. This does depend on the branch. The vine can take the life-giving elements only as far as the branch. What happens from then on depends on the branch. If the branch is really "abiding" in the vine and not just hanging there, the channel will be open to take what the vine has to give.

The *abode* illustration makes this clearer. When we are a guest in a home we could just be there, but lock ourselves incommunicado in our room. But that would not be abiding there in any meaningful sense. To get the most out of the experience, we need to avail ourselves of all that the host offers and give of ourselves unreservedly in turn.

It is unfortunately possible to confine the Christian religion to a mere static relationship. At conversion we become a branch, but it may go no further than that. We may go on living our lives as if nothing has happened. We are attached to Christ but we do not experience His life surging through us. This is sheer tragedy because it misses the whole purpose of conversion. There can be no fulfillment, no fruit that way.

Mutual Abiding

The challenge of Christ that we abide in Him is a two-way process. Perhaps we could put it like this: "Abide in Me and let Me abide in you."

It is apparently very much like the development of any desired friendship, most especially in courting. The man must take some initiative towards the girl he is interested in, usually by beginning to share with her some of his personality that he cherishes and maybe gently probing her heart. But there can never be any real mesh until she begins to move toward him. To make this possible, he will try to create an atmosphere of trust and friendliness in which she can feel secure enough to give a little of herself.

Before long, if the approach is successful, the personalities develop a kind of mutual abode, a private and unique world into which others cannot enter, a place where the inner need for love and friendship can rest.

The very language which Jesus uses gives some idea of the degree of intimacy and self-giving which is required. Like any other relationship with another, it involves a redirection of the personality.

A person alone is a law unto himself. He is conscious only of the needs of his own ego for satisfaction and fulfillment. Within the limits of his own circumstances he is free. But once he desires love or friendship, he has to take into account that he must sacrifice some of his freedom. His personality must be directed now towards the needs of the other person as well. In any relationship which is worthwhile, this restriction is amply repaid by the added dimension of fulfillment that comes from love.

Abiding in Christ calls for special redirection because it requires an alignment with a completely new philosophy of life, alien to what Paul calls the "natural" man. A child is born egocentric. His only interest is his own needs, and he tries to make everybody else subservient to these. He may not hesitate to snatch a piece of candy out of another child's mouth and plop it into his own, completely unmoved by the distress he causes. As time goes by we try to civilize him a bit, but this is only a thin veneer.

Christ comes along and staggers us by challenging us to a God-centered life which lays down the interests of the self entirely. He put it in all its stark nakedness once: "If any man will come after me, let him deny himself, and take up his cross, and follow me. For whosoever will save his life shall lose it: and whosoever will lose his life for my sake shall find it" (Mt 16:24-25).

To live with Jesus when he was on earth meant sharing His poverty, but this was not the real problem. It was the sharing of that utter self-giving. It is still the problem now.

But if we think that is tough, think of what He has to do. He has to come and live with us with all our selfishness and sin! Yet this is exactly what He wants to do.

But we do have to invite Him. He has to know that we really want Him in spite of that hard-to-take philosophy of life of

His. But when He does abide with us, we find that His presence so ennobles the soul that the life He offers doesn't seem so alien after all.

Abiding in Depth

A surprising feature of this verse 4 is that we are told to abide *in* Christ rather than *with* Christ. The apparent awkwardness of this construction makes it stand out. It could not be accidental. Jesus has a special reason for it.

When we look over the teachings of Jesus, we see that His use of *in* when we would have expected something else is not limited to this passage. In fact, it is widely used in His teaching on personal faith. Instead of saying that people must believe Him, He says that salvation comes from believing *in* Him (Jn 3:16), as we saw in the section "Total Committal" in Chapter 1.

Here the difference is between intellectual belief and that depth of belief which brings the total committal of the life. Just believing what He says is too easy because it calls for no commitment. There is nothing at stake. But as we have seen, the faith that brings Christ into the soul has to be much more profound. It is the kind of belief that makes us bet our whole lives on Christ. After we believe *in* Him, we are so convinced about all that He stands for that we give our lives unreservedly into His hands. It is like the difference between believing what an investment salesman says and actually turning our money over to him. Then we really believe in him.

Abiding *in* Christ calls for this kind of depth. To merely abide *with* Him is too casual. It implies a take-it-or-leave-it attitude. Perhaps it is like the difference between a woman living with a man in his home and a woman marrying into his home. In the former case, she is under no obligation. She can get up and leave when she wants. But when she marries him, she is not just a guest in the home, she is part of it. She has committed herself to the man to help him build his home.

Jesus made it clear that such a step should not be taken lightly. The cost should be fully counted at the start. His famous illustration was that of a man who wanted to build a tower, but Christ insisted that to avoid the humiliation of failure, he had better determine first whether he has the money (Lk 14:28-30). This makes sense.

The Christian faith has no place for those who want to use it merely as a ticket to heaven. You can't get by merely by entering into a transaction or signing a contract. What is done has to be done with the whole life.

But abiding in Christ is far more than a pledge to live His way. It calls for a committal to Him personally. He didn't say, "Abide in the Christian faith." He said, "Abide in Me." This, in itself, calls for added depth of committal. When we accept a cause, we commit ourselves only as that cause is affected; but when we dedicate ourselves to a person, everything goes with it. It has been said that a great deal of Napoleon's success was due to the magnetism which made personal devotees of his soldiers. The enemy soldiers were fighting for various causes, including their countries; but Frenchmen were fighting for Napoleon, and that made a world of difference.

The astonishing success of Christianity during the first century A.D. was largely due to the personal appeal of Christ. His disciples loved Him so much that there was nothing they would not do for Him. The accent must always be on Him.

Abiding in His Passion

There can be no merging of personalities in any friendship without a sharing of the deepest passions of the heart. We may believe and think differently from our friend, but we must be in tune with the emotions that move him. In the same way, if we are to abide in Christ, we must needs share the agonies of His soul.

The New Testament once and for all does away with any idea that God is impassive. Always He is the suffering God. Actually, it was not a new concept, for it occurs in the Old Testament, too. In the book of Hosea, God's anguished love for Israel is pictured in the prophet's misery for his wayward wife. But in the life of Jesus the truth is crystal clear. The suffering of the world seems almost to overpower His spirit at times. He weeps over the bereaved sisters in Bethany (Jn 11: 35), and over Jerusalem when He contemplates the awful fate ahead (Mt 23:37). Again and again we are told "he had compassion on them."

Calvary was the greatest instance of the suffering love of God. It has been compared to a volcano in eruption. As you watch the red-hot lava pouring out, you know you are getting a glimpse of what the heart of the earth is like. Calvary only lasted a few hours, but during that time the world saw the anguished heart of God erupting before the startled gaze of the very people who had contributed to that suffering.

The sad thing is that Calvary never stops, because God continues to suffer. He always will as long as the creatures He made also suffer.

The Bible picture is of a God who feels everything that we feel. No pain, no heartache, no sickness, no anxiety, no grief ever comes to our heart without stabbing His heart, too. The love of God is so great that He cannot keep away from sharing our suffering even when it is due to our own foolishness and wickedness.

In Philippians 3:10, Paul says that the great desire of his life is to know Christ, and one of the elements in this intimate knowledge he gives as "the fellowship of His sufferings." It is evidently quite clear to Paul that this is involved in abiding in Christ. It has to be.

We can't live with Christ without feeling the way He feels. The more we get to know Him, the more we love Him for the way He loves, and the more we find ourselves getting that way, too.

It soon throws a different light on sin. Before we share his heart we are apt to be tolerant of sin and excuse it, but when we sense the way He feels, it takes on a terrible repugnance. It hurts Him.

Abiding in this kind of love changes our attitudes to people. What happens to them becomes vitally important. Their troubles may not affect us personally, but they affect Him, and therefore we are necessarily personally involved too.

This is the cross that He asks us to take up.

Abiding in His Mission

Earlier in this century a newspaper man went to cover the devasting Thames floods. He found several officers of the Salvation Army there deeply involved in rescue work. They became his friends. Quickly that friendship drew him in until he was no longer just a reporter. He was in there pitching with the rest. Ultimately this experience led to his conversion, but the important thing here is that the man could not be friends with people involved in an urgent mission without becoming part of it himself.

According to the teaching of the Bible, God is a missionary. Theologians call His mission *redemption.* The only way we use that word now in everyday conversation is to speak of buying back something we have hocked in the pawnshop! If we were to use a happier and more modern term we would call it God's *rescue operation.*

That is what it is. People, because of their own folly or that of others, have slipped into the swamp of sin and its consequences. The result is unhappiness and hopelessness in this life and the next. Although this is not God's fault, His love will not let Him remain indifferent. He has to get in after them and rescue them.

The Bible is the story of that rescue operation down the centuries, an epic which reached its climax on the cross. Until then the rescue had been through men, but at Calvary He reached down in His own person and gave His life for those He wanted to save. Since then His Spirit has carried on His work through men once more.

We must not imagine that God's redemption is simply evangelism. As we have seen, evangelism is at the heart of it because conversion changes the heart where the root of sin lies. But He also wants to rescue from the consequences of sin. Jesus Himself preached the gospel but He did much more.

He went about doing good, rescuing people from the harrowing evils in which they found themselves.

To abide in Christ is to be obsessed with His own sense of divine mission, to feel the pull of human need and to involve oneself in meeting that need. This will mean that we are all evangelists seeking by all means in our power to win people for Christ. But it will also entail that we will follow Him into those swamps of human misery and rescue all we can.

This will be a very practical undertaking, for rescue cannot be carried out in general. If we try to rescue the world, we will rescue nobody.

A girl came down from the country to board with a Christian family in an Australian town. She soon found that there was not much Christianity there. They were religious but unpleasant. The husband and wife nagged at each other, and the two girls were like fighting cats. Selfishly they pushed the unpleasant chores on to the newcomer. But she did not complain and she did not criticize. Before long the love of her Christian witness was a beachhead in that enemy's camp. Within a year most of the unpleasantness had gone.

Christ needs beachheads like that everywhere. It is the only way the job can be done. It should happen wherever a Christian is.

The Shared Life

Someone has said that the human soul is like a homing pigeon. No matter how far you take it away, an inexorable inner drive will always make it try to fly home. The soul comes from God and can only find peace and contentment in union with God. But it is never a passive union. It means our spirit going out to God and His to ours.

The satisfaction is not in a state but in action. The mutual abiding is not a honeymoon retreat. It is a base for operation.

The joy of the Lord does not drop like dew from the heavens. It is the result of the fulfillment of the deepest needs of the personality. Someone has called happiness the pleasant emotional glow that comes when the personality detects that all its inner powers are being satisfyingly used.

It is a great mystery that God desires union with our hearts. But He does so, not for His own enjoyment, but so that He may find extra channels to others for His own rescuing love. For our own sakes as well as His, He will not allow us to remain inactive in the paradise of that union with Himself. His heart within us will drive us into action.

But just as we share His passion and His mission, He will also share our hearts' deepest desires. Not only that, but He will hound us on towards the self-realization we need.

The parable of the talents (Mt 25:14-30) underscores the sin of not expressing to the fullest all the potential that God endows us with. But this sin is not only in the record book in heaven. It is reflected in our psychological nature in frustration of spirit.

Man is not like an animal which with full belly can lie down in the sun and be content. Man has to have more than pleasant circumstances. His nature is like a coiled spring set by his God-given drives. These have to find realization, and only when they do can there be any sense of well-being.

Christ is within us to accomplish this. He will not allow us to be mired down by our laziness or petrified by our fears. Inexorably He will urge us to be the best that we are capable of.

At forty, Boris was a broken, defeated man. His marriage had exploded and his business gone bankrupt. He retreated into a near psychosis of self-pity, defeatism, and alcohol. But he had a friend who would not pity him and would not let him be. He nagged and hounded Boris to get up and get going. Boris insulted and abused him, but the friend would not be deterred. In the long run the persistence of love paid off, and Boris found himself again.

That is the way Christ is with us. He will sympathize with us in our troubles but will not brook our inertia or cowardice. We cannot continue to abide with Him unless our faces are always set towards multiplying our talents in the service of God and others. Once we are there, there is no escape from those piercing, beseeching eyes. He will make sure, regardless of the cost, that we are as expendable as He is and as fulfilled.

5

The Implications of Abiding

VERSES 4-8

Helpless Without Christ

In verses 4 and 5 Jesus describes the utter futility of the Christian who does not abide in Him. He flatly declares, "Without me ye can do nothing."

Now obviously this statement is relative to what Jesus has been talking about and is not meant as an absolute. Even an atheist is capable of good deeds and indeed may accomplish a great deal for his fellow men. All of us do many things, most of them good and useful, whether or not we abide in Christ.

What Jesus is referring to is the carrying out of the divine plan. God has a blueprint for every life and even for history. To the extent in which this is followed, the maximum usefulness is guaranteed. But we are not forced to accept His design. This is up to us.

When we do what the blueprint says, we necessarily accomplish something permanent, whether it is in our lives or the world of which we are a part. As we have seen, as far as our inner lives are concerned, abiding in Christ produces His fruit, what He intends.

Recently a friend of mine accidentally put diesel fuel into her Oldsmobile instead of gasoline. The intentions were good, but it was far from what the designers intended, as the results quickly showed!

Similarly, work for others or for society which is not in accord with what God plans is ineffective and may even be harmful. It is like a soldier in wartime having a crack at the enemy on his own initiative without regard to the overall strategy!

The need to be Christ-directed in our activity is graphically shown in an incident that occurred after the resurrection (Jn 21:3-6). The disciples had been fishing all night without success. Then in the morning when they were close to shore where fishing was normally hopeless, Jesus gave them a simple direction where to put down the net, and they had a bonanza.

This incident not only shows the difference that divinely directed activity makes. It also shows that real success can come from a most unexpected quarter. In the days of the book of the Acts, the fumbling preaching of the peasant disciples looked terribly insignificant in comparison with the great things going on in the world of Rome. Yet what they started not only replaced Rome but changed the history of the world. The difference was that they were Spirit-led and, therefore, in line with God's eternal destiny. Compare that with Alexander's meteoric achievement three centuries before. The whole known world saw his blazing star in the heavens, but his accomplishment for the good of man in the long run was pitifully small.

We tend to appraise events by the publicity they receive or by the numbers of people involved. God measures them by their significance in the long run of history. The dedicated mother who never preached a sermon in her life may raise a child whose influence for good may never die, whereas a famous woman may splash the headline for a time but leave not even a ripple for God behind.

This does not mean that while we are abiding in Christ we will be constantly getting supernatural messages of guidance. No. He doesn't usually work that way. To us it may appear that nothing is happening, but because we are in His hands, He is guiding us unerringly on.

There is no end to the excitement and significance that this gives to living. What we do is not immaterial. It has meaning and purpose. We are co-workers with God, weavers of destiny. In comparison with that, even the most flamboyant self-effort is, as Jesus says, "nothing."

Rejection by Men

In verse 6, Jesus goes on to warn that failing to abide in Him will cause us to be considered rubbish, and men will throw us on the scrap heap. The workmen will go through the garden, gathering up the dead wood and dry leaves and destroy them out of sight.

This is similar to what He has already said in verse 2, but not quite the same. There God is the judge, but here man is. There the reality of whether or not we belong to God is tested by our fruitfulness. Here, if we are not abiding in Christ, we will soon appear so dead and useless to people around that they will reject us and our message.

The Sermon on the Mount has a similar warning (Mt 5:13), although the metaphor is different. There it is salt. Jesus says, "Ye are the salt of the earth: but if the salt have lost its savour, wherewith shall it be salted? it is thenceforth good for nothing, but to be cast out, and to be trodden under foot of men."

The world has a great respect for genuineness but despises pretense. Only the real thing can command respect and can expect acceptance.

Many people find this unnecessarily discouraging. They are only too well aware of their imperfections and they dread being labelled *hypocrite*. Even worse, they cannot live with the thought that they feel that way about themselves. They feel that they would rather not profess to be Christian at all than let their Lord down.

But a man is not a hypocrite just because he imperfectly carries out the Christian obligation. He is a hypocrite only when he is not really trying and his heart is not in it. In my opinion, in these days, there are few people who are hypocrites. There is very little point in it anymore. There are, of course, many people who mean well and do badly.

These are the people (and this includes most of us) whom

God wants to help, and this is the purpose of this great message of Jesus in John 15. Christ within us progressively accomplishes what we cannot.

But the genuineness referred to here is more than just integrity in intention. It is whether or not the behavior is God-generated or not. The results of self-effort look the same, at least for a time, but it is not the real thing.

The big test is just that—time. Even the most emotional experience at a revival will quickly evaporate if it is not the real thing. But if God really has generated new birth within the soul, the ups and downs of emotional feeling will make no difference.

Probably the most detested subterfuge to hide a pseudo-faith is religiosity or piety. It ought to sound impressive to be mentioning God every half-sentence or so, or to be sprinkling the conversation with Elizabethan clichés, but it isn't. The average person can see through it like glass.

Fanaticism is a similar device to camouflage hollowness. The frustration of emptiness can drive the soul to change everybody else instead.

The search of the eyes of the world is far more penetrating now than ever before. They see through the artificial and quickly detect whether there is anything real underneath. At the moment the church is not doing too well under that gaze. Yet Christ Himself is as respected as ever. You cannot miss the fact that He is genuine. If we let Him have His way in our life, we cannot help being genuine too.

Prayer and Abiding

In verse 7 Jesus makes a startling tie-in with prayer. "If ye abide in me, and my words abide in you, ye shall ask what ye will, and it shall be done unto you." Statements like this have always had a special attraction for those who want an Aladdin's lamp, where the struggles towards achievement can be replaced by rubbing the lamp or using some other magic formula.

Such prayer is an affront to human dignity as well as a slight on the nature of God. It lowers man to the beggary of replacing initiative by seeking handouts, and it reduces God into an irresponsible tamperer with His own orderly universe.

God would never countenance any scheme by which we could take over His universe from natural law. Imagine what it would be like if the several hundred million Christians suddenly had this power, stopping and starting rain, changing the direction of the wind, willing food down like manna, striking dead those who didn't believe as they did, taking political power into their own hands. It would be an unspeakable bedlam.

It is obvious that prayer must not be looked upon as a resignation of responsibility by God or as an interference with order. Prayer cannot be alien to the universe. It has to be part of it. Instead of being an interference with His laws, it has to be part of them. Praying has to be as natural, and as supernatural for that matter, as sowing the seed.

The student who imagines that prayer can do away with the need for study is in for a big surprise. But he is in for a pleasant surprise when he discovers what prayer can add to study!

Also it would be foolish to believe that prayer could be so superficial as to be separated from the personality as a whole. This would be the case if it were possible to pray for things without experiencing any change in us. In a sense, it would be just marvellous if we parents could pray for our children and get them straightened out when they are veering off center, without doing any straightening out of ourselves. But it doesn't happen that way.

Jesus is making the implication here that prayer is something we do with the personality and not just with words or the mind. It is a way of extending the personality beyond that which it could normally reach.

This concept is present too in the story of the importunate widow (Lk 18:1-8). She couldn't win justice from the worldly judge except by such insistence that she wearied him. To her, this was no mere incidental request. Her livelihood depended on it. Consequently, she was driven to throw the whole weight of her personality behind it.

But even so, it is possible that with all the force of a personality behind a request, it could still be wrongly directed and outside the plan of God. What Jesus is saying is that there must be proper alignment of the personality before prayer can be successful.

However, as we have seen, abiding in Christ and being cleansed by His words tend to accomplish just this. The more we abide in Him, the more we are controlled by Him. If the control is total, then the prayers that we utter will reflect His wishes and successful answers will be guaranteed.

For a moment, let us go back to the blueprint illustration. God has everything planned to bring about the best results. Therefore, any prayer to alter that plan in any detail is doomed to failure. The only way in which God can conscientiously agree to a prayer is when it is in line with the blueprint. Abiding in Christ guarantees that.

But doesn't this make prayer superfluous? No, because as we have seen, God's blueprints are merely His recommendations. In fact, we probably seldom carry them out in full. It would be a different world if we did! What prayer does is to help to make God's plans a reality.

We do not know how this is or why God has made prayer so necessary. But He has. It is quite evident that unless we pray for some things, they will never be accomplished.

According to Jesus then, prayer is a responsible adventure in cooperating with God to accomplish His purposes. This way it takes on a significance which gives it both meaning and dignity.

God's Public Relations

It is in this kind of successful prayer, Jesus says in verse 8, that God is glorified. The King James Version here is not particularly clear. The Greek goes something like this: "In this my Father is glorified in order that ye might bear much fruit and in order that ye might be my disciples." The King James is ambiguous in that it could give the impression that God is to be glorified in the fruit bearing and in the discipleship. This certainly turns out to be true too, but it isn't exactly what Jesus is emphasizing. The "in this" is referring to answered prayer. It is this which glorifies God, and the purpose of God being glorified is greater fruitfulness.

The term *glorify* generally means bring credit to, make famous, cover with renown, but in the New Testament it has an added slant especially with regard to Christ. *Glory* means the full expression of deity. This Christ had to lay down to become man (Jn 17:5) and this He resumed again at His ascension (Jn 12:16). Jesus is God in disguise, but at times the veil lifts, and we get a glimpse of the full glory of His deity.

This is also true of God Himself. Because God is spirit and not flesh, He always seems to be hidden from us. The only way we can detect His presence is by His actions. But when things happen that exhibit His power, then we become aware of His deity and thus He is glorified.

Answers to prayer are particularly effective in glorifying God in this sense. I can remember that when I was a teenager, full of doubts about the existence of God, just how impressed I was by the instances of successful prayer, such as those of George Müller taking care of his orphanage in Bristol and Hudson Taylor providing for his mission in inland China. These men had put God to the test, and He had accomplished great things through them. In reading about their prayer exploits, to me God was glorified.

This is an obvious reason why prayer is encouraged in the Bible. It not only brings God into contact with human need, but it also gives people a glimpse of God in action. Now prayer is far more than merely making requests of God, but asking God for things is an essential part of it. The hymn expresses an important truth when it says, "Oh what needless pain we bear, All because we do not carry everything to God in prayer." It is not only pain and trouble that would be alleviated, it is the things we miss. Our lives are impoverished because we do not ask enough.

Some people hesitate to ask because it seems selfish. But wanting things for oneself is not in itself selfish. That is perfectly natural and is quite in line with the benevolence of God.

He wants to shower us with good things, which would not make much sense, if He didn't mean that we were not to want them too. No, wanting things for the self only becomes selfish when we proceed to get them at the expense of the welfare and happiness of others.

This added aspect needs to be stressed. God is glorified not only by His action in answering prayer but also by the evidence of His benevolence that this gives. He appears before mankind as a generous God bending over backwards to give good things to His children.

Seeing what God can do is always the best advertisement for the Christian faith. When we are so close to Him that we pray in accordance with His desires we become His public relations agents. He is a wonderful God. All we need to do is to let people know it.

Fruitful Discipleship

At first it seems surprising that Jesus should talk about Peter, James, John, and the rest conditionally *becoming* His disciples. After all they *were* His disciples and had been for a long while.

But there is a great deal of difference between being *called* a disciple and living out the implications of a disciple. It is something like being a student. If a person is enrolled in a college he can call himself a student, but that doesn't necessarily mean that he does much studying. This point would not be lost on the disciples.

The word *disciple* simply means learner. It is both amazing and sad to see how little the disciples really learned about Christ during His earthly life. In spite of His example and His teachings they could still quarrel about positions in His cabinet in an earthly kingdom, and when the crucifixion came it took them completely by surprise. Yet it is apparent that they memorized most of His teachings, because these were later recorded in the written gospels. Somehow very little of the message got any further than their heads.

Yet earlier they had probably nodded their heads knowingly when Jesus accused the unresponsive Jews of the same thing.

"This people draweth nigh unto me with their mouth, and honoureth me with their lips; but their heart is far from me" (Mt 15:8). They were oblivious to it, but we can see now that in so many ways they missed the significance of what He was saying by a million miles.

It was said earlier that disciple means learner and so it does, but there is more to it than that. Perhaps *cadet* might be a better word. A cadet not only learns but progressively puts into operation what he learns.

But the more theory deepens into practice, the more the cost in terms of risk. Just to believe what the master says takes little effort, but when it means selling all that you have and giving to the poor as in the case of the rich young ruler, it becomes a much tougher proposition.

Discipleship in the manner prescribed by Jesus means going out on a limb and the courage to make that gamble takes all the faith that we can dig up. This is where answered prayer is such a tremendous boost. It enormously adds to our conviction that God is real, and the more we can sense His presence, the easier it will be to risk all that we are as His followers.

We notice that Jesus ties fruitfulness in with discipleship as a product of answered prayer. The reason is easy to see. The willingness to be disciples comes from the eagerness to be entirely His, and as we have seen earlier, this is what allows His life to flow through us and produce the fruits of the Spirit. Discipleship and fruitfulness go together. Thus prayer produces a double harvest.

There is just one more point in this verse which is worthy of comment. In the Greek, where Jesus talks about becoming "my disciples," the *my* is emphatic. This personal touch adds to the significance of discipleship. A disciple tries to reproduce the qualities of the Master. If he is successful, then in time, he should become a pretty fair copy of the original.

The amazing thing that He is promising is that we can become reproductions of Himself. He possesses us so entirely that we can become "Christs," never attaining to His level, but nevertheless sufficient to make discipleship take on a revolutionary significance. Paul says, "For me to live is Christ" (Phil 1:21), and by that I think he means that because he (Paul) is living, Christ is living again because He indwells and lives again through the apostle.

6

Gifts of the Spirit

VERSES 9-13, 17

Benevolent Love

In verses 9 through 13, Jesus expounds on two of the fruits of the Spirit which can be expected to develop from our union with Him as branches to the vine. These are love and joy. It is no coincidence that these are the first two fruits in Paul's famous list in Galatians 5:22-23. In 1 Corinthians where he talks about the gifts of the Spirit, Paul says love is the greatest gift of all (1 Co 12:31; 13:13).

Love is a most ambiguous word in English because we do not have separate words to distinguish between such things as sexual love, friendship love, and benevolent love. Fortunately Greek does, so it is easy for us to tell here that Jesus is talking about benevolent love, as is also Paul.

Benevolent love has been called the love of the will rather than of the emotions. It means the outgoing of the personality in the interest of the welfare and happiness of others. As such, it goes far beyond sentiment or feeling and is completely unrestricted in its application.

Emotional love is not like that. It is necessarily directed towards special people. Our psychological makeup is such that we are not capable of loving more than a very few people this way at any one time. When we try to spread ourselves further, the emotion is either lacking in depth or becomes a mawkish pretense.

Many Christians find it a great relief to understand this difference. They feel guilty because they don't love everybody like they love their children or their friends. This is impossible and is certainly not required. But although we do not have to feel the same about everybody, we do have to be prepared to act towards everybody in the same self-sacrificing way as we do our loved ones.

Supposing we come across a personality misfit in real need. He may be abrasive, self-pitying, unpleasant. For sincerity's sake, it doesn't make sense to try to get "lovey-dovey" over him. But the Christian faith does require that we become so concerned about him that we do what we can to help him.

However, there is a danger with this love of the will. It can become too easy, degenerating into mere heartless duty. This can occur if we are not personally involved in our emotions, when the act of service is somehow carried on outside of ourselves.

This is the kind of thing that can happen when those we try to help are "cases" or "patients" instead of persons. You get the same kind of impersonal touch when some evangelists say they are "saving so many souls." If their task is to go beyond mere statistics, they must save *people*.

Benevolent love, the *agape* of the Bible, is the *want to,* as well as the *have to* or the sense of moral obligation. It is the ability to include a little piece of oneself with every gift of love, every action of service.

Albert Schweitzer, above many men, seems to have caught the admiring eye of the twentieth century as an example of Christ-like, self-giving, benevolent love. It does not seem to have been any real hardship to him to leave his brilliant career in Europe to become a medical missionary. He wanted to. His acts of service to the needy Africans were not time off from his own personal life. They were his life, the source of his joy and fulfillment.

That is what Jesus is talking about. But it doesn't come

easily. If it is to be the natural outreach of the personality, it has to come from the God who is love, the fruit of His Spirit within.

The Chain Reaction of Love

In verse 9, Jesus states that benevolent love should start with God, go on to Him, and then spread to us. "As the Father hath loved me, so have I loved you: Continue ye in my love." It should be like atomic fission which is a chain reaction. The initial bombardment starts others, and these do the same until the expression goes beyond all bounds. God wants His impact of love of Christ to multiply until the whole of the human race is showered by it.

In line with what has already been said about benevolent love, Jesus implies here that love is not something that we simply bask in. It is a way of acting. God acts in a certain way towards Jesus, He towards us, and then we towards others. It is something that requires a decision of the mind and a response of the heart. There is nothing passive about it.

It is always a little puzzling to have Jesus refer to Himself as the recipient of God's love when He is God. But the Bible is always careful on this point. It never confuses Jesus with God. Jesus is God but the Scriptures do not say that God is Jesus, rather "God was in Christ" (2 Co 5:19), which preserves His deity and yet nevertheless acknowledges that He is a person in His own right. Since He is a separate center of personality, God can direct His love towards Him and He can consciously be aware of it.

In turn, He expresses benevolent love towards the disciples. In fact, He has no alternative because to receive God's love is to transmit it. It isn't something that can just be absorbed. The capability to receive God's love necessitates a certain state of the heart. The receiver has to be in tune with it. Unless the heart has the same obsession to express itself in benevolent love towards others, it cannot even pick up the signals.

In the same way, the disciples could not merely passively bathe in the warmth of Christ's love. They have to be transmitters too. That is why He says, "Continue ye in my love." They continue in His love by continuing it, and they can continue in it in no other way.

Now, in a sense, nothing can separate us from the love of Christ (Ro 8:35). It is being transmitted all the time. But that does not mean we are sensing it all the time any more than a radio is receiving all the time even when the transmitter is operating. That depends on the radio.

Love is not a substance like some kind of spiritual gas. It is the name we give to a certain kind of action directed by very special attitudes. Whether it is God, Jesus, or the disciples, love is the soul in action. There is a pleasant sense of elation that accompanies this which is often confused with love. But this kind of love far surpasses any emotion. It is the personality on the march in service to others. When Christ tells us to continue in that love, He means to persevere in that march.

There is a quantitative aspect to this love too. The passage serves to imply that to the extent in which the love of God and the love of Christ is shown, we must continue in the adventure of loving. Superficially regarded, this appears to be too staggering to be realistic. Who can love like God? But a more careful thought makes us see that what Christ means is total self-giving in love. This is an attitude rather than an achievement. If, to the very depths of our souls we are totally given over to this life of love, as far as we are capable, then the committal is total and not even God can go beyond totality. We then love as He loves.

Commandments and Love

In verse 10, Jesus says that the way to continue the love experience is to keep His commandments. He says, "If ye keep my commandments, ye shall abide in my love; even as I have kept my Father's commandments, and abide in his love."

If we are not alert to His way of thinking and His overall philosophy of life, we might easily assume here that He wants us to make a list of the rules and regulations He has laid down, follow them explicitly, and then expect to be rewarded by being allowed to abide in His love. It is made very clear in the gospel records that He was not interested in that kind of legalism. He broke the commandments about the Sabbath by allowing the disciples to husk the grain in their hands and struck back at His critics because they put the cart before the horse. God never intended man to be burdened by Sabbath regulations. He intended the Sabbath to be a benefit to man (Mk 2:27). The happiness and well-being of man was the important thing. On this principle, He praised David for breaking the commandment not to eat the sacred bread in the temple (Mk 2:25-26). David's need overruled even that.

The most far-reaching example of His irritation with regulations occurs in Matthew 22:34-40. Here He summarizes the whole Old Testament moral code in the dual principle of love for God and for others. Paul echoes this principle in Galatians, in his fierce abrogation of law in favor of grace and freedom.

Regulations serve a useful purpose as moral guides during immaturity, which was what the Old Testament period was. But mature people do not need rules. They need principles of action which they can freely apply according to the dictates of their own conscience. Christianity is a religion of maturity.

A good illustration of this is in the moral obligation not to steal. In the Old Testament this was handled by the command "Thou shalt not steal" (Ex 20:15), but in the New Testament a Christian does not steal, not because of any commandment, but because he doesn't want to. The principle of love has replaced the letter of the law.

It is obvious therefore that Jesus does not mean laws or regulations when He speaks of commandments. Proof of this is found in verse 12 where He cites loving one another as one of His commandments. Love cannot be commanded in the ordinary sense of command. It has to be generated.

What Jesus means is that our motives are to be activated by the principles of His teaching. Where there are cases that look like regulations, they are illustrations of an underlying principle. Slavishly following the regulations could easily cause us to violate the principle involved. For instance, if our right eye offends us should we pluck it out as He apparently directed (Mt 5:29)? Or is this just an illustration of an attitude by which we are willing to suffer physical loss rather than meet spiritual disaster? Giving all our goods to feed the poor might easily generate spiritual pride in some, rather than be surgery for greed as it was with the rich young ruler (Mk 10:21).

People are so different and circumstances so diverse that no system of rules can ever fully cover moral obligations. The clever casuist can always make evasions on a technicality. But there is no legalistic bypass in the principle of self-giving. There may be varieties of applications but always it will be obligatory on us to do that which is in the interests of the other person.

But Jesus meant something more than this. He believed that the whole of life should be subject to the personal guidance of God. Because He loved God, He kept Himself completely at the disposal of this guidance. This not only maintained His attitude of self-giving, but also directed it to whatever God wished. Jesus knew that even the most sacrificial self-giving can be fruitless and wasted unless it is used wisely.

As disciples we should be eager to receive this same guidance on the details of our lives. To the extent in which we obey these commandments we will be abiding in His love.

Joy that Remains

Earlier in this chapter it was mentioned that the emotion of joy promised by Jesus was second on Paul's list. But the treatment by Jesus is somewhat different from Paul, for He thinks of it as a by-product of love rather than as a separate fruit of the Spirit. It occurs in verse 11 as part of His exposition of benevolent love.

This is what He says: "These things have I spoken unto you, that my joy might remain in you and that your joy might be full."

The "these things" that Jesus is speaking of presumably refers generally to His great message about His indwelling power but specifically to what He is teaching about love. It is noteworthy that He doesn't tell His disciples to abide in His joy as He does about love, but rather makes a promise that they will have the joy remaining in them.

What He is implying seems to be this: "Express yourselves in benevolent love as I do and you will find joy such as I experience welling up and remaining in you."

It is evident that this kind of joy is not a mere synonym for happiness in general but is rather *love-emotion,* the emotional glow that is generated by self-giving towards God and others.

Happiness in general can be a most transient feeling ebbing and flowing with the ups and downs of circumstances. It is easy to be happy when things are going fine and to be gloomy when things are bad. But having one's sense of well-being completely at the mercy of happenings not under our control is neither satisfactory nor is it consistent with human dignity. It is so superficial that it is a far cry from the abundant living that Christ said He had come to give (Jn 10:10).

Reference has already been made to the prime desire of all human beings to find fulfillment in self-realization. If this is not achieved there is an immediate corresponding emotion—frustration. If it is attained there occurs a warm glow inside, the emotional sign that the personality is fulfilled.

Now Jesus takes over this psychological fact by promising realization through benevolent love. In so doing He is giving direction to the personality in its drive for fulfillment. Knowing human nature as He does, He is aware that the greatest satisfaction, and therefore the greatest joy, comes in the achievement of self-giving love.

This *is* something which is under our control, for whether we live in His kind of love or not depends on a voluntary decision on our part. There is nothing transient about this kind of joy. It will remain as long as we are living according to His life prescription.

Now this joy will not enable us to enjoy toothaches or taxes or flat tires, nor will it oust the moods which come from the variations of our endocrine gland hormones. What it does entail is that we will retain the basic glow of well-being even when we are harassed by the various nuisances of life.

In view of what Jesus has said earlier, it will not be too fanciful to add that when He says "that my joy might remain in you," He means something a little more intimate than just His kind of joy. Since He is within the soul and it is His Spirit who is generating and directing the self-giving love, then it is His joy we are feeling. Our hearts are reflecting the glow in the very heart of God.

No wonder that He can predict that our joy will be full.

His One Commandment

After this little digression into the joy that accompanies love, Jesus in verse 12 makes another stab at the legalism which would kill love. He says, "This is my commandment, That ye love one another, as I have loved you." In the Greek, the "my" is emphatic, so perhaps we can paraphrase what He is saying something like this: "The scribes and the rabbis all have their codes of ethics and systems of morals worked out in the tiniest detail but I have only one commandment—just love one another. If you want to do that with all your hearts, you will always know what to do."

Already in this chapter we have taken a good look at what Jesus means by commandment and found that to Him it is the compulsion of the soul to do what is right rather than anything like regulation. In that reference He speaks of love in general and most especially, the love that motivates His life and action, but here He is applying it to their own personal relationships with one another.

Living together with people always involves strain. No matter how much we love one another, our separate egos are always striving for satisfaction, recognition, and fulfillment. This wouldn't be so bad if it could be done impersonally but it never can. The presence of others brings barriers to our self-realization and we become competitors for our fulfillment. The result is ego war.

We tend to use each other to gain advantage in the struggle.

We argue, not to find truth, but to win an ego victory over the other. We criticize so that we can decrease his importance in our eyes. We palm off the unsavory tasks on to him making us appear as kings and him as a servant. We resent his successes because this makes him appear better than we are. We knock his ideas no matter how good, because we want to belittle him.

It isn't a very nice picture but it is a realistic one, and it is common among Christian couples, families, and even churches.

Now, as we have seen, Jesus recognizes the ego principle, the drive for fulfillment. He doesn't want to kill this by any means. The personality has no force without it. The trouble is not with the drive but with its direction. In other words, He wants us to have ego satisfaction, but in a way which will give us lasting satisfaction without hurting others. His plan is simple. Get your achievement in service.

It works this way. Suppose I find myself in an argument. My immediate reaction is to try to flatten my opponent, thus gaining a quick ego victory. The way of Christ would be to try to make the encounter a satisfaction to him. Instead of trying to demolish him, I recognize and admit the elements of truth in what he is saying. I still may have to disagree with him, but he soon gets the idea that I am trying to contribute something to him as well as receiving something myself. When the discussion is over, I have the satisfaction of having made him happier and his life a little richer. That means far more to the ego than winning an argument.

This is only one example but it shows how the principle of love works. The main principle is to get our kicks out of contributing to the other person.

It is most noticeable that when the apostle John was old, he kept coming back to this love-one-another principle. Tradition has it that he was close to a hundred years old when he wrote the first epistle of John. At that vantage point, he seemed to feel that unity and harmony between persons are of the greatest importance. "Little children, love one another," is his recurring refrain.

In all our personal relations we still need to emphasize this. Accuracy, efficiency, orthodoxy, these have their place but they are of far lesser importance. If we have the pressure of the heart of Christ within us we will be driven to put first things first.

The Extremes to Which Love Will Go

Verse 13 is one of literature's famous gems. "Greater love hath no man than this, that a man lay down his life for his friends." Jesus seems to use it here almost as an afterthought. It is as if He is reflecting on the wonder of benevolent love and the joy it brings. When it is driven by total self-giving, it does not know where to stop. It has no brakes. It will not even balk at death itself.

These immortal words were spoken before Calvary, but we cannot help but interpret them in terms of what happened there. On the cross He gave Himself for the sins of the world. He laid down His life in death so that we, His friends, might live forever.

Usually we think of His death only in terms of the sovereignty of God—Jesus was submitting to the divine will. This is quite true, but from what He has been saying here we can detect another kind of compulsion—the compelling force of His own self-giving love. He could not do anything else but lay down His life; otherwise, He would have been false to the love that obsessed Him. He could not draw back anymore than a mother can hold back from the churning, angry, death-threatening waters, when her child has fallen in.

There quickly came a time when discipleship was put to the ultimate test. To profess the faith meant cruel martyrdom. It is to the eternal credit of the disciples and their followers that they did not shrink from this awful cost. The thing that amazed their persecutors was the joy with which they laid down their lives for their Friend.

But perhaps here we are too quick to assume that laying down one's life means laying down one's life in death, although that is the usual meaning of the idiom. It is spectacular and requires enormous faith. Yet it is not as difficult, or as necessary, as laying down one's life in living. You can die in a second under the executioner's sword or in hours at the hands of the torturer, but to lay down the life in living may take a lifetime of self-sacrifice.

Some of the early Christians missed this point. The glamor and fame of martyrdom so attracted their imagination that they eagerly sought it, even going out of their way to bring themselves to the attention of the authorities. There was a rumor that if you died a martyr you received double reward in heaven. The church leaders firmly denounced this thirst for martyrdom. The task of evangelism needed dedicated *living* Christians.

It is only in this emphasis that these great words of Jesus can have relevance to most of us today. We are not called upon to die for the sake of our Friend or for our friends, although we should be willing to do this. But there is tremendous need for us to place our lives at His and their disposal.

A few years ago a nationally renowned retired public official in Australia gave his services as a janitor to a needy Christian seminary. A New Zealand doctor with a promising lucrative career at home volunteered to serve as a missionary in India. An American priest went to live in border slums to win wayward Mexican youth. Greater love hath no man than this.

But it can be even simpler than this. There is the mother who refrains from anger and self-pity to uplift her family. There is the student who denies himself many of the pleasures of youth to study for a more useful future. There is the girl who brings harmony to her home by sacrificing her attempts to bulldoze her own way over others.

It is all a matter of self-giving. If He has really gripped our hearts, love, even to these extremes, will not be too difficult. It will be the way we want to live—above ourselves.

7

From Slaves to Friends

VERSES 14-15

SLAVE AND LORD

IN VERSES 14 and 15 Jesus takes his disciples an important step forward in the life they are to share with Him. They are to be promoted from the status of slave to friend. (The Greek word translated "servant" means slave.) The implications of this transition into being friends of Christ are just tremendous.

Our life in Christ and His in us as pictured by the analogy of the vine and the branches was never intended to be static. It starts in embryo and progressively matures. It is always a process of becoming. Christ is permeating the soul to the extent with which we abide with Him. As He does so, we become like Him, and His purposes in us are progressively fulfilled, thus making us eligible for greater responsibility. The highest status to which we can attain is as His friend and confidante.

The first stage of our relationship with Him is slavery or servanthood. Actually, we never leave this. We are always His slaves called to be His friends. The apostle Paul is a good illustration. Few people have ever risen to the heights of intimacy and friendship with Christ that he attained, yet to the last, one of his most beloved titles was "slave of Christ" (servant of Christ).

The difference is that in the first immature stage we are

slaves only; in the second stage we are slaves elevated to be friends of the Most High.

To our modern ears the term *slave* does not have a favorable sound. A slave is one who no longer has the power of self-determination, one who is completely expendable and at the disposal of his master. When this master is a human being like the slave, the relationship is degrading and an affront to the dignity of both. But when it is between God and man the situation changes. Instead of having our freedom limited, it is enormously extended. Instead of having our powers of action repressed, they are multiplied to the nth degree. Instead of having our personality submerged, it becomes merged with God to find a far greater self-realization.

It is something like a boy laying aside his freedom to follow his every impulse so that he can go to college and train for a useful future. It is like a man throwing away his shovel to drive a bulldozer. It is like giving up bachelorhood to marry a loving and helpful woman.

Freedom is relative and absolute freedom an absurdity. Our choice is not for total freedom or none, but for a choice of freedom that will enable us to more fully realize the best that is within us. Slavery with Christ means limitation, but it is the kind of limitation a train has in having to confine itself to the railroad tracks. If it decided to take off in some direction other than on those tracks, it would be freer in a sense, but it would never go any place.

We can choose to be slaves to ourselves, the most bitter tyranny of all, or we can be slaves to Christ and find real freedom.

As we have seen, Christ demands an unconditional surrender to Himself and absolute control over our lives. The Bible message on this is very clear. There can be no halfway position, no compromise. Christ made it clear that we cannot serve God and mammon (Mt 6:24). He will not take us at all unless we are willing to become His slaves. He knows He cannot permeate the soul if there is any resistance to Him.

Friend and Friend

The previous discussion has shown that slavery to Christ is not an unhappy state to be emancipated from, but a happy, enriching privilege that is always going to be ours. But while the Lord will always demand this submission to Himself, He wants to add this greater opportunity whereby we also know him as friend with friend.

In verse 13, Jesus has already given us an insight into what He means by *friend*. It is a kind of relationship which is so deep and close that we are prepared to lay down our very lives for the friend. This goes far beyond mere acquaintance, the associations where we pass the time of day, but in which there has been no significant self-giving. It is nice to have acquaintances like this, but because of their take-it-or-leave-it nature they do not have much permanent effect on our lives.

The friendship that Jesus means here is the binding of two personalities into such a union that each feels the hurts of the other, and each has a stake in the welfare of the other. Perhaps the key to the criterion of such a friendship is involvement. We have invested our personality in that of the friend. There is a kind of identification with him so that what happens to him appears to be happening to us.

At the time Jesus was giving this message to the disciples, this kind of depth was not yet true of their relationship with Jesus. He was calling them friends in the hope that they would ultimately measure up to this dizzy height, but in actuality they had a long way to go. At this stage, although they were obviously very attached to Him, they still wanted to use Him. They hoped He would set up an earthly kingdom, and they wanted to be in there on the ground floor when the cabinet positions were being offered, as witness the ugly lobbying of the mother of James and John (Mt 20:20-28).

After He left them, all that changed. They were no longer interested in feathering their own nests. They were oblivious to the suffering and sacrifice they were called upon to endure. Their great obsession was to carry on His work and not to let

Him down. They had graduated to His concept of friendship.

Necessarily, such a truth as the indwelling life of Christ within, which Jesus is expounding in this chapter, does fill us with a sense of excitement and anticipation as to what He can do for us. This is as it should be, but we must not let it stay there. If we are to become His friends, the emphasis has to be on what we can do for Him.

Fortunately, what He can do for us and what we can do for Him are not mutually exclusive possibilities. His enrichment of our lives can make us far better servants of His. Where the step forward occurs is in our attitudes. In His own words, it is where our heart is (Mt 6:21). We are His friends if we consciously think of what these good gifts can do for Him.

It is something like this. Suppose a person who has a close and dear friend buys a sports car. One of the things that immediately enters his mind is just how much his friend is going to enjoy that car with him. He will find himself planning outings and adventures with the car involving his friend. The new car experience will be friend centered. With a more casual acquaintance he would not think the same way, but his new car would not have anywhere near the same satisfaction.

Essentially, friendship is sharing life—its joys and sorrows—with someone else. Friendship with Christ takes this to the highest plane, where we become immersed in everything that is upon His heart.

At His Disposal

When Jesus says, "Ye are my friends, if ye do whatsoever I command you" in verse 14, He is making it clear to the disciples that this friendship is not something they can take for granted. It is not a status they have attained as a reward for faithfulness at the slave level. It is rather an opportunity for a higher and more rewarding kind of action. Whether they remain His friends or not is going to depend on the extent to which they are at His disposal.

There is something of this subtle distinction in the saying "A friend in need is a friend indeed." Friendship is the personality in action towards the meeting of the other person's need. The only way in which friendship can be other than action is when the personality is poised to take helping action the moment it is needed. In any real sense, friendship ceases when that readiness fails or is withdrawn.

This poised-spring state of the personality is typical of deep friendships. It remains even when there is little personal contact. In the pioneering days of the West, when mobility was difficult, there were wonderful stories of rugged friends who had not seen each other for years, yet who downed tools and took off to help when a sudden call for aid came. No questions were asked, no appraisal of the worthiness of the appeal, or even of the legality of what was asked. The fact that the friend had called for help was sufficient. Of course, not all friendships were that deep, but that kind of devotion did become quite a tradition. Jesus wants friends like that.

A similar no-questions-asked attitude was required of military men during World War II. In projects like that of the atomic bomb even full generals were kept in the dark for security reasons. They had to be prepared to follow out orders no matter how silly or unnecessary they seemed. Friendship with Christ calls for the same attitude.

Now in verse 15 Jesus promises that He will share with the disciples all that the Father tells Him, but this does not mean that they will know the reasons for everything they are called upon to do. Often He may not know this Himself. The Scriptures strongly suggest that as a man He did not possess absolute knowledge. He had to grow like everybody else (Lk 2:52). His supernatural knowledge was a gift from God and was not of Himself (John 8:28). He, too, had to be willing at times to follow blindly the orders that came from higher up, that is, from his heavenly Father.

Being absolutely at His disposal is primarily for His sake. He has given us the task of carrying on His work, but we won't be very effective unless we are doing it under His direction. Even the best-intentioned efforts on our part can make it worse for Him if we are not careful. The trouble is that we cannot see the future and yet the success of many of the things we do now depends on those unseen events. But God sees all the tomorrows as an open book and can guide us accordingly. There is nothing mysterious about such guidance. God will be almost automatically guiding us if we are abiding in Christ, and if we have this eager willingness to do whatever He commands.

This kind of submission to His will brings rich dividends to us, too. Although His work and mission have to be His primary aim, our satisfaction and well-being are important to Him, too. Indeed, it is part of His mission, for every person is vitally important to Him. But also it is through fulfillment that we grow, and as our abilities expand, our usefulness to His kingdom expands, too. So while we are at His disposal and in His hands, He keeps an eye on us personally, guiding us where our best interests lie and away from the shoals where we could be hurt. Most of this work on our behalf is completely unknown to us. It happens behind the scenes in the circumstances that affect our lives.

It pays to be His friends, even though that is not why we are His friends.

Taking Us into His Confidence

Verse 15 is full of tender intimacy as Jesus explains to the disciples that all the secrets that have come from His own communion with the Father are to be theirs because they are His friends. "Henceforth I call you not servants; for the servant knoweth not what his lord doeth: but I have called you friends; for all things that I have heard of my Father, I have made known unto you."

In other words, just as they are to become His friends by placing themselves utterly at His disposal, He is going to treat them as friends by sharing with them even His inner life with God.

Now He is doing this because He needs friends with whom He can share. We all do. It isn't possible for us to exist amid the pressures of living with people without building up all kinds of tensions inside and accumulating a lot of hurt too. This can soon prove too great a burden for us unless it is shared with someone we trust. Because Jesus was human, too, He longed for friends to whom He could bare His heart.

However, it is not this element of sharing that Jesus is primarily referring to. It appears that mostly He wants friends with whom He can share the wonderful news about living that God is making known to Him. This is a touching human trait. We are made in such a way that we can't bear to keep good things to ourselves. Jesus is no exception.

This verse is somewhat puzzling because we cannot find any real startling truths that Jesus did tell His friends, the disciples, not even in all the years that followed. We would rather expect solutions to some of our vexing theological problems: the Trinity, the problem of evil, what the hereafter is like, and so on. But if He ever said anything on these teasers, it never was recorded. Yet if there had been any such disclosures, I like to feel that they would have been put in the Bible, because we are His friends, too, and He wants to share with us as well as the early disciples. It is apparent that Jesus had little interest in this kind of enquiry. He was not a philosopher, given to academic speculation. His great interest was human beings and their living in harmony with one another and with God. The truths from the Father were about living—the Sermon on the Mount, the parables.

It gives point to what Jesus is saying when it is remembered that the Sermon on the Mount was a talk to the disciples (Mt 5:1), and that the parables were directed to them, too. These magnificent and revolutionary truths which were to change the history of the world were not proclaimed on the housetops. They were given in quiet, private talks to His friends.

These disclosures to His friends did not end with His earthly life. That would have been tough on us, because we would never have had these intimate moments when He could share with us the gems from God. It would have made our lives the poorer, too, because we constantly need new truth to meet our changing conditions. If we are abiding in Him, He will always be telling us new secrets.

When I read the Bible and get a flash of light on some ancient truth so that it inspires my life, it is His gentle love that is behind it. When someone says a word of kindness that touches the spot in my aching, hurting heart, it is His voice I am listening to. When I am impelled to undertake some new and worthy task, however small, I am sensing the touch of His Spirit. When in my human concern I put a loving hand on the shoulder of someone in distress, He is sharing with me what He wants to do through me. He is communicating to me what He is hearing from the Father.

Occasionally these messages from above are revolutionary enough to change the history of the world. Think of what He shared with Martin Luther about reform in religion, to William Carey about taking the gospel to the heathen world, to Lord Shaftesbury about social injustice, to William Wilberforce about slavery. In His own time in history these great disclosures are made to some friend of His. For most of us, this is not our destiny. But a true friend has no false pride. It is sufficient for us to sit at His feet eager to listen to anything He has from the Father and to act on it at His bidding.

Developing the Friendship

The sharing in friendship can never be one-sided, however. The depth of relationship that Jesus has in mind implies two hearts completely open to one another. Jesus had no secrets from His disciples. He wanted them to hide no secrets from Him either. He needed the sense of closeness that came from their confidences, and they needed the release that such sharing brings.

We need this, too, and not always are there earthly friends available to us to whom we can unburden our hearts. But He is always available. Sad to say, few of us bother to confide in Him, although His heart is longing for this expression of friendship on our part.

Psychologist Robert Thouless once said that Protestantism, in doing away with the confessional with priests, intended to replace it by confessional with God, but in practice, it never turned out that way. Most Protestants never unburden to anybody, resulting in unnecessary mental ill health. It doesn't need to be like that.

In a sense, we can feel much more secure when we share with God the load on our hearts, because we can confess everything without a shadow of fear. Even the dearest earthly friend may turn weak and betray our confidence or may fail to love us enough when He finds out how bad we really are at times; but He is never like that.

But this friendship with Him is far more than a mere confessional. It is the sharing with Him of every area of the life, of whatever we are interested in, significant or trivial. This, too, is the essence of continuous prayer.

Early in this book, considerable attention was given to prayer as asking for things. This is part of any friendship. Friends like to be asked to do things. But most conversation between friends is not of that nature. It is usually aimless, free association of ideas, often about the minutiae of living. The content of the conversation is not important. It is what it does that counts. It enriches the friendship and living at the same time.

Our friendship with the Lord is impoverished if we confide ourselves to purely religious matters in our conversation with Him. Just imagine how bored we would become if we had a close friend who only talked to us about religion! God is no more interested in religious things that He is in secular matters. In fact, He doesn't make that distinction. To Christ all things were sacred.

Children start off with His viewpoint on this, but we soon ruin it for them. A child's prayer is about strawberry jam, his toy train, the boy who cheated him at marbles, what the weather will be like for the picnic planned, whether his teacher is going to be crabby. If in saying grace when we have company, he thanks God that there is none of that awful spinach tonight, we are a little embarrassed and coach him later as to what he *should* pray about. This is a great pity.

Jesus once said that unless we receive the kingdom of God as a little child we shall in no wise enter therein (Mk 10:15). I think that He had prayer in mind, too, when He said this. He would like us to have the openness and naturalness of a child.

If we are troubled with wandering thoughts in prayer, it does not mean that we are wicked. It just means that we are not praying about what we are really interested in. The wandering thoughts are the real prayers of the heart. We do not need to choke them off. All that is required is that we should share them with Him.

We should never be ashamed to talk with Him about the so-called trivia of life: the football game, the weather, how trying the traffic is, the blueness of the sky, the irritations of the job, how fast the lawn grows, the trouble down at the city hall, the book we have just read, how nice that last vacation was, the rattle in the car. This is the kind of water that He loves to turn to wine because of what it does for our friendship with Him.

This is a friendship which is always available. He doesn't go off on a vacation or move to a new town. He is always there because He is within us. He is always as close as the vine is to the branches.

8

Predestined to Serve

VERSE 16

Chosen by Christ

"Ye have not chosen me but I have chosen you" (v. 16). In these words Jesus emphasizes the dignity and significance of discipleship. The disciples may have imagined that they took a great deal of initiative in getting to be His followers. Certainly some of them did (Jn 1:37). What Jesus is saying here is that this destiny was chosen by God long before they had anything to do with it. They simply fitted in with His plans.

This doctrine of predestination has a very strong place in the Bible, but unlike some of its adherents, the Scriptures never present it as a force overriding human initiative and freedom. Instead, it is intended to be an incentive to action and an encouragement to responsibility.

Perhaps human responsibility may be illustrated by this story. A native who knows nothing of ships is invited to travel on a missionary lugger. The next morning he goes on deck and sees only a vast expanse of ocean. It might appear to him that he is now completely at the mercy of wind and wave, but someone explains to him that this is not so. There is a captain who is guiding the ship to a very definite destination. Then he is shown how to steer the lugger and after a while is left at the wheel while the captain does something else. In his inexperience he may drift off course a bit, but always the captain is not far away, making sure that they reach their intended destination.

There are some people who believe in fatalism, that everything about life is cut and dried, that God has predetermined everything about our lives, and that there is nothing we can do about it except be resigned to it. This is certainly not the view of the Bible. It is constantly exhorting us to follow the wishes of God and telling us of the penalties if we don't. This would have no meaning if we were just robots.

What this means is that Peter, James, John, and the rest became disciples through no accident, yet neither was it inevitable. They were chosen by God from the beginning of time, but they themselves had to accede to that choice. The rich young ruler was chosen, too, but he turned the opportunity down (Mk 10:21-22).

Neither was our conversion an accident, no matter how fortuitous it may have seemed. God planned it that way. His foreknowledge enabled Him to see all the myriad events that led up to that encounter with Himself. But this did not guarantee our surrender to Him. Maybe there were many previous encounters which were unsuccessful.

Now that we are Christians, we are being groomed not merely for being Christians in general but for the special tasks which we are to carry out in this life. This preparation is part of a master plan involving both us and our circumstances, which goes back over untold centuries.

There is heavy responsibility in this truth. It means that nobody can do the job for God that I am doing, nor as well as I am capable of doing it. Of course others might do it as well as I am doing it, but this is only if I am not doing the best that I am capable of. No other person in the world is precision-tooled for my God-given tasks as I am. The sad aspect is that if I fail, or even if I do not realize my maximum potential, nothing can quite make up for it. There will be an irreparable gap in part of God's plan.

But being chosen of God is wonderful, in spite of the awesome responsibility. We ought to feel as proud as an appointee does when the President of the United States offers him a Cabinet position. We are co-workers with God Himself.

Established and Authorized by Christ

When Christ says "and ordained you" we are likely to assume that He is no longer speaking to us but rather to priests and ministers. But this is not so. The word translated "ordained" did not have an ecclesiastical meaning in those days. The disciples did not have to go through an ordination service or anything like that. He called them, they followed, and that was all there was to it. (Mt 4:19-20). The concept of a difference between priests or ministers on the one hand and the laity on the other, was a much later and perhaps not a particularly happy development. Of course, the church did have teachers from the start, but I am referring to the idea that some Christians are given special rights in religious duties that others do not have.

By *ordain* in this verse Jesus seems to mean that He is establishing them in their task of being disciples and also has given them His authority to act on His behalf.

The establishing involved two processes. The first was training them in an understanding of His message, His methods of teaching and general operation so that they could be His heralds, as they were called to be in the incident of the sending forth of the twelve (Mt 10:5). This was never a mere matter of mechanics, for it was more than learning. He sought to give them confidences in the presence of the indwelling Spirit who would put words into their mouths (Mt 10:19-20). Training could not prepare them for every situation, but the Holy Spirit could.

The second establishing process was the maturing of their personalities. At first they were changeable, unconvinced, unreliable, apt to abandon Him if the going got real tough as it did at the arrest (Mt 26:56). Slowly, patiently, but surely, He was placing a set in their attitudes which would make them solid rock. The success of this part of His work in their lives did not become evident until after He died.

Their authorization to act on His behalf was nowhere so difficult, because it needed only a word from Him; whereas the other required their cooperation in a slow process of personality change. Yet it must have been a great boost to their egos—to be the spokesmen and servants of the Most High God.

God is eager to carry out the same work of establishment in us. Certainly we are all as eligible as the disciples were. Even in His day they were not the only ones called to be His heralds. There were the Seventy, too (Lk 10:1). Apparently, also, there were some independent emissaries who were not attached to Jesus in any way, and who roused the ire of the disciples for that reason (Mk 9:38-39). It is evident from the book of Acts that every convert was expected to be a herald of the gospel. This was the genius of New Testament Christianity. The spread of the Christian message was everybody's responsibility, not just that of a few paid professionals.

It may be objected, too, that the words of Jesus here are in the past tense—"I have ordained you"—indicating something already accomplished. This is certainly true, but it is not all past. It is something like a president being appointed to a university. He may be set up in his position by the trustees, but actually being a president by carrying out the implications of his job is something else again.

We are ordained as disciples of Christ to represent Him in this world. Now we have the task of really representing Him. He has given us His authority, His message, and His Spirit, but He has done much more. Instead of leaving it to us after this, He stays with us Himself to help us in the task. As we have seen, this is implicit in this whole message of the vine and the branches, but He has also said so explicitly. When He gave the Great Commission He added, "And, lo, I am with you alway, even unto the end of the world" (Mt 28:20).

Destined to Go

"That ye should go." Jesus goes on to say that the goal of all this divine choosing and planning is action. When you come to think of it, there is little room for a life given solely to contemplation of Christianity. It is always "go!" "Go . . . and preach the gospel" (Mk 16:15), "Go, and do thou likewise" (Lk 10:37). In this the Christian faith is in sharp contrast with some ancient religions which advocate retiring from action and feeling.

Because of this emphasis, we can see how sadly the monastics misunderstood their faith. Their intentions were very noble. They were ready to give up everything for God, particularly the life of action and involvement in living. But they could not have been more wrong. They were needed in that world of men they were leaving. Instead of retreating into the deserts, they should have been advancing with the hosts of God to rescue those for whom Christ died.

Without action Christianity quickly deteriorates into mere sentiment. There is nothing more weakening to the character than being moved by inspiring preaching and then doing nothing about it. Always the time comes when we have to get up and go.

It has been suggested that one reason why God allowed the savage persecution to break out against the first Christians in Jerusalem was that they had begun to like it too well there. In the midst of the great things that were going on there, they had forgotten that they were to go into all the world. The persecution made them go anyway, and so the Word spread far beyond the confines of the sacred city.

As we have seen earlier, we can never be content with inaction anyway. In our hectic, rushing world nothing seems more attractive than that quiet, remote, sleepy village in Mexico, but this is an illusion. It is nice to get away from things for a time, but after a while the inaction drives us mad. The number of alcoholics in some of those idyllic spots to which people have tried to escape is quite large, and we can guess why.

Sheer human inertia is one of the biggest enemies of spiritual progress, or any other progress for that matter. We just don't get around to doing the things we ought. People dream all their lives of achieving cherished objectives but never do. We do not like to exert ourselves too much.

The opposite to inertia is drive, and it is amazing what can be accomplished through drive. This is what kept Columbus going until he discovered America. It is what made crippled Glen Cunningham go on to become the greatest track athlete of his day. It is what inspired Father Damien to go and live among the lepers. Most of us do not have such a propelling force as a native endowment, but Christ does and He is within us. Christianized countries develop far more quickly than those lands where the older faiths are predominant. The Christ within a man's heart breaks down his inertia and drives him into action.

The other enemy of action is cowardice. Sometimes it is fear of circumstantial consequences, but this is not nearly so common as fear of failure. We are reluctant to poke our ego noses out for fear they might get bloodied. This is realistic enough, but Christ demands action at whatever the cost.

When I was a teenage Christian, I told a Salvation Army officer that I would not go with him to help in an open-air service because I was afraid of making a fool of myself. He told me that I could never expect any real Christian victory until I was prepared to do just that. Someone has said that we must be prepared to be fools for Christ's sake. This is very true.

If we are dedicated to Him, we will fear neither failure nor harm. We will recognize that in His great work of redemption, everyone is expendable and we will want to put our own lives on the altar. It is not just evangelism or other religious duties. It is His whole mission among men. We may enjoy the inspiration of the great moments on the mountain tops, but inevitably we have to gird up our loins and go to the valleys where His needy, loved ones are.

Permanent Fruitfulness

Earlier in the passage Jesus has said a good deal about becoming fruit bearers, and here in this verse 16 He raises the matter again. A close translation of the Greek of the relevant words would be "in order that you yourselves might go and that ye might bear fruit and that your fruit might remain."

Apparently Jesus wants to save any misunderstandings about the "go" part. It would be easy for the disciples to fall into the trap. He has been trying to save them from earlier; that is, to imagine that the Christian faith is mere external activity, whereas it is essentially the outliving of the indwelling Christ.

It is possible that I may be separating the go from the fruit-bearing too much in this paraphrase. It might read "in order that ye might go to bear fruit" where the "go" could be left out altogether, such as when we say "I'll go and eat dinner" when we mean "I will eat dinner." However, without splitting hairs too much, I prefer to think that Jesus is meaning the going and the bearing fruit as two distinct developments. Earlier when He speaks of bearing fruit He does not use the go construction, so by adding it here, we can assume He means something a little more.

In other words, He is anxious that we get up and go, but He does not want the frenzied activity of self-effort; He desires His heralds to be attractive advertisements for the message they bring. It is His aim that His disciples exemplify the truths that they are proclaiming.

The problem in His mind here does not appear to be eagerness for consistency between message and living. He often vigorously criticized the Pharisees for this hypocrisy, but not the disciples. Rather, His aim seems to be propaganda, similar to what He has said about answered prayer. The message is about the reality of an unseen God, in whom people are being asked to entrust their lives. They need tangible evidence to back up this gamble. God's transformation of the weak disciples provides this. God may choose His elect from among their listeners, but this will be totally academic unless they are convinced enough to respond by seeing what God can do. The fruits of the Spirit present this evidence.

The implication for us is that our faults, such as bad temper, greed, selfishness, bad habits, rather than being merely a poor witness (which they certainly are), are an opportunity to show what God can do. If an evil thing in our lives is conquered and replaced by a good thing, that turns out to be a much greater witness to God's power than if we had been good all the time.

But in this verse, Jesus is emphasizing a new slant in this fruit bearing. The fruit has to remain. It has to be permanent. We can readily see the point in the case of the disciples. To say the least of it, they weren't a particularly promising bunch. Their weaknesses would be only too well known. Now those who knew them would not be too impressed by any sudden change because anyone can become a nine days' wonder under the spell of a new experience. Whether it lasted would be the test.

This whole verse is about God's predestination, so this would seem to imply that God deliberately chose the disciples because of their weaknesses. If they had been nicer specimens, they wouldn't have suited God's purposes and would not have been chosen to be the followers of Jesus in His earthly life. In the language of some contemporary television commercials, they were excellent before and after examples of the product Jesus was selling to the world.

This is greatly encouraging when we look at our own weaknesses and our utter unfitness to bear the name of Christ. The worse we are initially, the more challenge we are to God to prove what He can do once we abide in Him. A Christianity peopled by naturally good persons would have little evidential value. Weak people permanently changed make the world sit up and take notice. It is worth noting that almost all of the Bible characters were like that.

The Magic of His Name

As Jesus proceeded on this topic of the purposes He had in mind in choosing the disciples, their minds must have been staggered at the wonder of it all, and at the last item they must have felt like the favorites of an oriental monarch. "That whatsoever ye shall ask in my name, he may give it you."

There are overtones in this of moments like Belshazzar's lavish promise to Daniel (Dan 5:16).

Of course, as we have seen, Jesus has already dealt with this matter of success in prayer in verse 7, and this is a repetition, but in a slightly different context and with an added thrust of meaning. Then it was successful prayer as a by-product of abiding in Christ; now it is as part of the unravelling of the sovereign will of God. In verse 7 abiding is the condition. Here it is the use of His name.

This kind of repetition is characteristic of Jesus. He likes to mention a truth, usually in a brief and graphic form, then leave it and take up some other aspect of truth. Later He returns to it in almost the same words as if He hadn't said it before, only this time He may take it a little further. The impact of His teaching is like a tide coming in, as the waves advance and recede only to advance again. Apparently here He wants to thoroughly infiltrate their hearts with the majesty of just what can be accomplished in prayer.

In studying this second stab that He makes at prayer, we should keep in mind what has been said already about the earlier reference to prayer, that success in getting prayers answered depends upon our prayers being answerable. They must fit in with the divine plan. Everything else would be arbitrary and confusing.

Now Jesus is talking about the divine plan directly and explicitly places prayer as part of it. But now He indicates that making prayer in His name is the key to alignment with God's will.

At first sight it looks as if He is giving us a verbal, magical charm which only needs to be repeated to open the windows of heaven. This would make the art of successful prayer a merely mechanical thing, and nothing could be further from the mind of Christ than that. Even the enemies of the kingdom of God could parrot the words to bring about evil events, for the promise appears to be unconditional. *Whatsoever* is the all-inclusive term used. If Jesus had meant this as a charm—an open sesame to God's power—it would have been the most irresponsible thing any man ever did, because here is a power greater than the atomic bomb.

But experience quickly shows that such an interpretation of His meaning simply refuses to work in practice. Even the smallest child has tried it out, asking for valuable and much desired toys in the name of Christ, but without avail. It simply does not work. It never could, without reducing the world to chaos.

Yet we still cling to the faint hope that it might work "just this once." But witness to this is the fact that almost all formal prayers still finish with the words "in Christ's name, amen."

Praying in Christ's name is not a formula but an attitude of the heart that determines the content of the prayer. The trouble is that in English, a name is simply a handle. Names are chosen because they sound nice, or because we want to commemorate a relative or some other admired person. Many of our names did have meanings once, but usually they are not known to us now. To the Hebrews it was different. The name was a meaningful expression reflecting character and attitudes. They did not always live up to their name, but the significance was there.

The closest we get to it in English is when an erring child is scolded by the family for "ruining our good name."

The names of God, for this reason, always had a special sacredness. Once *Yahveh* (Jehovah) was so sacred it dare not be pronounced. The name of God refers to His whole being, that which makes Him what He is. Therefore, if we succeed in praying in the name of Christ, it means that we have so identified ourselves with His person and all that He stands for, that even our prayer requests have come to coincide with His desires. That kind of prayer cannot miss.

From this we can see that He is teaching us that successful prayer is not changing God, which is as impossible as it would be undesirable. It is changing us so that we have come into accord with the divine plan. Jesus says He has chosen us for this very purpose.

9

The Backlash from Evil

VERSES 18-20

Hated by the World

From verse 18 on, the message of Jesus takes on a sinister note. Until now He has been dealing with the outreach of the benevolent love in their hearts as they abide in Him. Now He has to warn them that love has it opposite—hate—and they must be prepared for the hurt it will bring. It is the inevitable backlash to love from evil.

He brings in this thought with His usual dramatic suddenness. "If the world hate you, ye know that it hated me before it hated you."

In view of the Christianized society in which we live, this warning appears at first sight to be out of date, a reaction to the bitter opposition He was receiving from the Pharisees. Nowadays, being Christian brings little threat of punishment and seldom any hostility of any kind. On the contrary, it more than often heightens our prestige and improves our reputation; so much so, that candidates for public office like to make it known that they are church members.

But even taking into account the greatly changed environment between the first century and now, and although overt hostility from people or society is rare, the hatred against the message of Christ is as great as ever. It is just that it is deeper and much more subtle now.

A careful study of what Jesus means by *hate* and the *world* shows that He had in mind something more than mere popular or eccelesiastical opposition.

There is one clear instance that shows that by *hate* Jesus does not mean that emotional reaction which we associate with the word. You will remember that Jesus once said, "If any man come to me, and hate not his father, and mother . . . and his own life also, he cannot be my disciple" (Lk 14:26). It is obvious here that He does not want us to feel hate, that is, animosity towards them. It is the hate of the will rather than the hate of the emotions. He wants us to be willing to put the kingdom of God first. He would not have us shirk our responsibility to parents. It is the dedication of our attitudes to Himself that He is after. If one of the disciples loved his parents so much that He couldn't bear to leave them to follow Him, even when he would not be put in jeopardy by this, this would be wrong. On the other hand, if he loved his parents with all his heart but nevertheless left them to do what He felt to be right, that would be true dedication. This is the hate that Jesus means.

This is quite similar to the way Jesus treats love. As we have seen, to Him *love* is not mere sentiment or emotion, It is the benevolent set of the will.

The term *world* is also used in a special sense, not only as something that hates us, but as something we should hate. This is particularly clear in the first epistle of John when he says, "Love not the world . . . If any man love the world, the love of the Father is not in him" (1 Jn 2:15). Yet we must not hate people (1 Jn 2:9). Also we certainly should not hate the material world, because God made it and made it good (Gen 1:10). He is neither referring to people nor things but rather to the attitude of people to things. There is a spirit or attitude present in the world which is antagonistic to Christ's message of benevolent love. This is the evil that prostitutes God's good gifts to merely selfish ends and resents anything that challenges this self-centeredness.

The animosity of the Pharisees was an expression of this

worldly spirit. The message of Jesus threatened their vested interests, their pride, their security. Their devouring of widows' houses (Mt 23:14) and the like was revealed in all its naked ugliness when the light of His teaching about benevolent love shone on it.

Our world is not so much hostile to the message of Christ as indifferent to it. But the prevailing attitude is the same, which is to put self first. This will always make the devoted Christian feel that he is swimming against the tide. If the world in this sense were always outside of us, the problem would be simpler; but it is inside us, too, and is even in our churches. The result is trouble, friction, disharmony.

Jesus is helping us to recognize just what we are up against, but He is also softening the blow by saying that He has to meet the same thing. He was in no privileged position. He understands what we are going through.

Not Loved by the World

In verse 19, Jesus continues the thought in a slightly different way. "If ye were of the world, the world would love his own." Being in harmony with the spirit of the world and aligning ourselves with its attitudes would end the opposition. While we swim downstream we have no problem. The current is with us. It "loves" us. It is only when we begin to swim upstream that the trouble begins. Then the current "hates" us.

The love of the world for its own is not a personal love any more than its hate is a personal hate. Even if I find myself in the company of a group of people who are completely disinterested in Christ I will not usually find them ganging up against me personally. But I will feel like a fish out of water. They too may feel uneasy in my presence. The result may well be that although they have not deliberately ostracized me, the effect is the same. They may even wish I would leave and be glad when I do. Thus they have all the characteristics of hate for me but without any emotion of animosity.

This uneasy state can very well erupt into violence and certainly did with the early Christians. The heathen world found them so unlike itself that the isolation was very marked. Then when troubles came, the pagans turned on the Christians in actual hate. As Jesus saw so clearly, their unconscious minds were hating them anyway.

The world loves its own because it is comfortable with its own kind. The problem is seldom a matter of real wickedness because evil in too vivid colors makes the world uneasy. What the world seeks for is an easy, comfortable, self-pleasing existence with a minimum of interference. People who fit in with that philosophy of life are loved. Those who do not are hated.

The world does not mind a certain amount of external activity as long as it is not too demanding. Drives for social and community betterment it takes in its stride, so also religious observance. It objects only when the heart has to be changed, when the will has to be laid down in surrender to a higher will, when there is a threat to the self.

It follows that no matter how diplomatic and tactful the dedicated Christian is, he will be a source of irritation to the world. He may be the most popular man in town, yet if he is doing his job as a Christian, he can't avoid building up resentment against himself. People see in him the image of Christ and the comparison with their lives builds up unconscious (or even conscious) guilt.

This hidden, inner resentment comes out at odd times in criticism, because when we criticize, we are trying to lower a person nearer our level so that the difference between us doesn't seem so great. Then we don't feel quite so bad on account of our own moral failure. If we can't get at a person directly, we may resort to nit-picking, attempting to make issues out of minor points of theology, political views, oddities of personal behavior. The enemies of Jesus were constantly nibbling away at Him in this way. As He warns, we must expect the same treatment.

There is no way of avoiding this enmity between Christianity and the world except by watering it down until it loses its offensiveness to the spirit of the world. But this negative effect is no mere necessary nuisance. It is part of the plan of God, because through it God speaks to the heart.

Apparently most permanent conversions occur after quite a period of what has been called subconscious incubation. This is the progressive building up of impulses in the unconscious mind to a point where they can be triggered off into a personal decision. It appears that the heart has to be ripe for conversion. The inner guilt that is built up by the impact of lives abiding in Christ provides a constant bombardment of the unconscious mind and adds greatly to the incubation process.

Not of the World

In the next few words of this verse 19, Jesus discusses the nature of the isolation of the Christian community from the world. "Because ye are not of the world, but I have chosen you out of the world, therefore the world hateth you." He makes it even clearer in John 17:15-16. "I pray not that thou shouldest take them out of the world, but that thou shouldest keep them from the evil. They are not of the world, even as I am not of the world."

The essence of this teaching is that He does not desire physical separation from the world of people but spiritual separation from the spirit of the world.

Since the very beginning of Christianity there has always been some feeling that the community of Christ should be physically separate from the non-Christian world just as Israel was rigidly isolated from the world of its day. This is sometimes due to spiritual pride—that we are too holy to have our skirts touch that kind of dirt. Sometimes we are too fearful of contamination by the world, or even worse, of being drawn back into it.

This is the very reverse of what Jesus intended. He Himself was no ascetic or recluse; in fact, He was criticized for His social activities (Mt 11:19). Where the people were, He was too: weddings, feasts, synagogues, highways, market places, and homes. He ate with them, drank with them, slept with them. His talks with them were largely about the simple matters of everyday living.

Yet He considered Himself "not of the world," and He wasn't. His absolute dedication to God and the utter surrender of His self to the needs of others put Him into an altogether different country from that of the world. He was forever an alien to the spirit of the world.

The command "come out from among them, and be ye separate . . . and touch not the unclean thing" (2 Co 6:17) must be interpreted this way. It is calling for a spiritual withdrawal, not for a physical ghetto.

The truth is that we can't get away from the world by physical separation, because the spirit of the world is also within us. The hermits of the fourth century rushed away into desolate areas far from the world they knew, only to find that in that artificial isolation the power of the world within their hearts was far stronger than its pull in the world of men.

This does not mean that some physical separation at times is not necessary. It is. The Christian besmirches his testimony when he participates in wrongdoing. This can be equally true when he is merely present during un-Christian conduct, even though he does not take part. Unless he protests, he is an accessary after the fact.

Provided that the Christian is not "of the world," he is needed in the world; otherwise, the message of Christ would never be known. Our churches provide little real opportunity for evangelism because they contact so few people. Those who do come to church see Christianity in a very limited aspect, only its formal religious expression. The real impact is made in associations with people where they live, in their jobs, their games, their community, their homes. When we mix with them in these areas, they see the faith in all its aspects because we are living right there with them.

If we are truly abiding in Him we cannot be anywhere else except with people because that is where He always is. Neither can we be of the world either, because He lives within our hearts, and there is no room there for both Him and the spirit of the world.

Sharing His Persecution

In the Sermon on the Mount Jesus explained that the source of evil acts was always in an original state of the heart. Murder came from anger and adultery came from lust. (Mt 5:21-22, 28). Thus it is a small step, as we have seen, from the passive state of hate by the world towards the Christian to actual overt acts of violence. This development was very rapid towards Jesus. Since a slave can expect even worse treatment than the master, the disciples had better look out!

"Remember the word that I said unto you, The servant is not greater than his lord. If they have persecuted me, they will also persecute you" (v. 20).

Persecution means something more than bad treatment. It has also the significance of being hounded. Occasional acts of malice do not need much motivation, but when we dog a person with persistent ill treatment, we are being driven by an inner spring of hate. From what has been said earlier, it can be seen that the Christian is in just this kind of peril. The impact of the dedication of his life produces inner guilt and this, in time, must lead to conversion or malice. If it turns bad, we can expect it to be persistent.

It certainly was like this with Jesus. The beauty of His life showed up the Pharisees in all their hollow pretense, and their hatred was not just a passive thing. It was a burning emotional animosity. They were so incensed that they were like dogs constantly biting at His heels. The crucifixion became inevitable.

What Jesus is saying is that the world will have less compunction against persecuting us. A citizen will be much less hesitant about criticizing a private than he will be a general; but if the man at the top is attacked, the lesser fry can expect little mercy. In Jesus' day this was especially true with slaves who could be treated like dogs anyway. If therefore the master was evilly dealt with, his slaves could expect no mercy at all.

Apparently persecution is inevitable. "All that will live

godly in Christ Jesus shall suffer persecution" (2 Ti 3:12). In the political and social background of the early church this was quite inevitable even in the sense of persecution by physical violence. We may not have to suffer torture and death for our faith now but the underlying hate of the world sooner or later must find its expression in persecution, although the form may be much more subtle now.

A Christian salesman who had been quite an outstanding success in his work asked his boss why he had been passed by for promotion. He was told frankly that vice-presidents of that company had a public relations responsibility and his not drinking with clients made them feel bad. A high school girl who felt that indiscriminate petting was inconsistent with Christian discipleship lost out to a far less eligible girl who was not so virtuous, when an election for cheerleader came up. A real estate salesman lost a hefty commission to a less scrupulous colleague when he found he would have to tell a few unpleasant facts about a house for sale.

But persecution not only comes in acts of discrimination like these. It is the price the Christian has to pay for belonging to an unpopular way of life. Those who feel guilty about their lives in comparison will have an unconscious set against him which will cause prejudice no matter how fair people try to be. This is part of the cost that the Christian must count on.

Since the world is more an attitude than anything else, we must not assume that persecution is going to come from non-Christians only. The world is also present in the hearts of fellow Christians and may impel them to act in un-Christian ways at times.

A girl who had had the experience of unmarried motherhood before becoming a Christian was forced by fellow church members to give up the Sunday school class she was teaching. A minister who invited a Negro fellow minister home to dinner had an expected salary raise rejected. Terrible things can be done in the name of Christ at times!

It will save us from unnecessary disillusionment if we remember that the world is primarily a confrontation between God and evil, a vicious battleground in which no holds are barred. If we are squarely on Christ's side, we cannot expect the enemy not to level his biggest guns on us at times. He did on Jesus!

Sharing His Acceptance and Rejection

After this rather sobering thought about persecution, the message takes a slight upbeat: "If they have kept my saying, they will keep yours also" (v. 20). But even this statement carries a negative side: if they rejected Christ they will reject the disciples also.

The argument Jesus uses here is that the disciples must expect their message to be treated the same way as His was. If the world is prepared to accept what He says, then it will accept the message when the disciples say it, and (presumably) vice versa. Now He is not getting off this topic of the backlash from evil. Rather He is explaining a particularly painful form of it.

A man's message, if it is from the heart, is a product of his own personality and cannot be separated from it. Preaching is truth through personality. It is this personality medium which makes possible transmittal from person to person. If the message is accepted and wrongly used, or if it is rejected, then the messenger feels slighted as a result.

Every preacher knows only too well this connection between personality and message—the gloom that comes over the spirit when the sermon turns out to be a dud or when the people's disinterest becomes only too obvious. Every parent knows it—the heartache that ensues when advice given to a child is rejected.

But the way Jesus frames it here, it looks as if He might be looking at the bright side—the pleasure that comes when the message is accepted. There may be an element of this present, perhaps to offset the unpleasant things He has had to say, but the context makes it difficult to believe that this is His main thrust. He is talking about the way evil is going to hit back at them, so somehow even this acceptance must at times harbor hidden hurt. It may be received but not kept in the manner intended.

An illustration comes from the life of Martin Luther. His message was eagerly accepted by thousands of German peasants, but much of it had little depth. One of the results was the Peasant's War bloodbath which so harrowed Luther's soul that he wished he had never preached at all. Jesus had experiences of this Himself, such as when His supporters wanted to make Him king, the very reverse of what He wanted.

It has been even worse since He left the earth. Those who have accepted His message have made a monolithic institution which has to spend more time and money on preserving itself than on the purpose for which it came into being. Even theology which was intended to be a satisfying intellectual dress for our experience of Him often becomes degraded into a fight among brethren. All this must bring great grief to His heart.

If this happens to Him we must be prepared for the same. The Sunday school class may appear to be taking in what we are saying, but most of them may drift off in time. Even when we have done our best to train our children and seem to have been successful, we can still experience the grief of seeing them do the wrong things. Evil never lets up and never gives up when it appears that we have been successful at first.

But Jesus did experience outright rejection of His message. As a matter of fact, during His lifetime that was mostly the case. This shows just how powerful evil is when it can effectively block the message of the Son of God. He had little to show for His three years' ministry when He finished. He had started with twelve disciples and finished with eleven, an eight-and-a-half-percent loss. If He had been a pastor today, most likely He would have been advised by His officers to move on! In the incident of His weeping over Jerusalem (Mt 23:37) we get a glimpse of how agonizing this rejection may be.

When people reject our message and our efforts, it is hard not to be discouraged. I sometimes wonder how William Carey kept on going those hopeless beginning seven years in India when he failed to win even a single convert. But he did.

Perhaps the example of Jesus can help us in another way not specified here but which is nevertheless true. If we can expect our message to be treated as badly as His was, we can also expect our words to bring forth fruit in the long run as His did. "Cast thy bread upon the waters: for thou shalt find it after many days" (Ec 11:1).

Yes, we can expect the sharp pain of the backlash from evil, but being a Christian is worth it many times over.

10

How Good Reveals Evil

VERSES 24-25

What Ignorance Does

In verses 21 through 25 Jesus turns His spotlight on evil actions and shows that they may be actually generated by good. You get an indication of this even in the Old Testament where God is said to be responsible for evil. The encounter between Moses and Pharaoh is a good example. There we are told that God hardened Pharaoh's heart (Ex 14:8). As a result he refused Moses' demands and had his armies destroyed. At first sight, it looks as if God hardened the poor fellow's heart and then drowned him for it, which seems hardly fair.

But there was nothing mechanical about it. The hardening came because he did not respond to God's demands. If he had surrendered, there would have been no hardening. Yet if there had been no encounter with God there would have been no hardening either. So you can say God hardened him all right. But the hardening was his responsibility, not God's. In similar circumstances Moses too had an encounter but responded, so you can say God softened his heart. Pharaoh, like every other human being, had to face the fact that there would be moral decisions to make which would result in sin or righteousness. In this sense, good does cause evil but is not responsible for it.

In verse 21 Jesus says, "But all these things will they do unto you for my name's sake, because they know not him that sent me." This is reminiscent of another remark in the first epistle of John: "He that loveth not knoweth not God; for God is love" (1 Jn 4:8). Jesus is saying that the unloving action of those who persecute the disciples is only possible because they do not know the God of love.

This is another case where English lets us down somewhat. The word *know* here has a depth of intimacy which would not occur to us when we used it. To us *know* means having acquaintance with or intellectual knowledge about someone. It can have that meaning in the Bible too but not in contexts like this.

It is worth remarking that in the Old Testament the word *know* is a term for sexual intercourse, as when it says "And Adam knew Eve his wife; and she conceived" (Gen 4:1). This is the meaning in its extreme form where two people are united in the love of sexual embrace.

In the nonphysical sense, the word refers to such a merging of personalities that each person can predict the other's behavior. You get this kind of thing when a wife hears that her husband has become the victim of some false accusation. She says, "My husband? Oh no! You don't know him like I do. He's absolutely incapable of anything like that."

It is the same emphasis in Philippians 3:10 where Paul yearns, "That I may know Him." It sounds silly, doesn't it? Paul knew more about Christ than any man alive, so what is the point of saying a thing like that? To Paul there was deep significance. He longed for an ever increasing union with Christ so that His knowledge of Him would transcend the academic. It was that deeper knowledge that made the great apostle not only able to write about the majesty of love in 1 Corinthians 13 but also to practice it throughout a long lifetime.

The fact that Paul was still seeking that knowledge when he wrote to the Philippians quite late in his life shows that knowing God or Christ is a progressive experience which must be diligently pursued. It helps to know about Him, but that is never enough. It helps even more to practice the kind of life

He lived and proclaimed, but there is still further to go. We must constantly seek Him in our hearts as they go out in love to Him, sharing His passion for those He came to save. The more we know Him like this, the more impossible will evils like malice become. It can get to the place where the only possible response, even when they hate and hurt us, is love.

Removing the Cloak

In verse 22 Jesus teaches that the persecutors have revealed their real sinfulness by rejecting His message and reacting with such violence. "If I had not come and spoken unto them, they had not had sin: but now they have no cloke for their sin."

Now He certainly doesn't mean by this that they were sinless before He came to preach to them or if He hadn't come they would have remained sinless. (This, incidentally, is a good example of the rule that we must dig deeper than what the Bible *appears* to say. The real meaning may be very different.) The final clause "now they have no cloke for their sin" shows that He means that His message uncloaked what was there all the time.

The theological expression *original sin* implies that the germ of sin is within all of us. But to become actual wrongdoing, it has to be hatched. This usually takes something to trigger it off, some circumstance that puts pressure on us.

Jesus says His message does this. It reminds me a little of some of those science fiction stories after Hiroshima, which played around with the idea of monsters being spawned by the effect of atomic energy radiation on living cells. The Word of God is like that. If we don't respond, it is likely to make monsters out of us.

We see this effect sometimes when a man is under conviction of sin at an evangelistic meeting. Normally a quiet, lovable person, he may become irritable, bad-tempered, abusive, and blasphemous. What happens is that the preaching has made him feel guilty, and that can really make a person mad.

In the epistle to the Romans, Paul has a good deal to say about imputation of sin (e.g., Ro 5:13). By this he appears to mean something like our modern word *indictment,* being pronounced guilty of sin. It is a legal term, whereas sin itself is an action word. Thus, though a person does something wrong, he may not be indicted or found guilty in a court of law. For that to happen, the act has to be shown to be a willful deed with full knowledge of its wrongness. Thus we do not imprison little children or mental incompetents. Paul means that God imputes guilt when a person's knowledge of his sin makes him morally responsible.

Jesus is explaining that His life and work give people the knowledge of good and evil. They see their duty clearly, and they are forced to take action about it. If they refuse to do the right thing, they have no excuse before God. They are guilty in His eyes.

It would seem that Jesus feels that His message is uncloaking in two senses. First, it is removing the excuse for sin by making the evil nature of the deeds perfectly evident; and second, it is stripping the sinful nature of the heart so that it appears naked to the world at large.

It might seem that a cunning person could avoid this guilt by avoiding the Word of God. Some do try this, but it is no way out. The very avoidance is evidence that he knows that there may be something wrong, and this implies the responsibility to find out what it is.

The disciple who is anxious to abide in Christ will bare his breast to the Word regardless of the pain it may bring; for the Word that reveals the cancer also destroys it, if we respond as God intends.

I knew a man in whom was discovered a case of cancer so developed that the doctors could do nothing for him. He was asked why he didn't come in for examination earlier. "I was scared that I might have cancer," he said. That man could have been saved if he had responded sensibly to his fear.

This uncloaking never ceases. The closer we get to Christ, the more the sin will be revealed. It is like a shirt after being worn for a day—the closer it gets to the light the dirtier it appears. Paul at the end of his life bemoaned the fact that he was the "chief of sinners." But the good thing is this: the uncloaking is also the way to spiritual health.

Hating the Father

The sin of hating or persecuting Christ or His disciples is more terrible than it appears. Jesus says that it amounts to hating the Father Himself. "He that hateth me hateth my Father also. . . . now have they both seen and hated both me and my Father" (vv. 23-24).

The persecutors of any age are reluctant to accept this truth. They would like to isolate their human victims and hurt them without injuring God in any way. Not only are they afraid to strike at God because of the consequences, but most of them don't want to hurt Him because they feel they love Him. Jesus is saying that this kind of distinction is an illusion. You can't hit your brother without hitting God.

Jesus spelled this out in no uncertain terms in His famous "inasmuch" passage where the sin is neglect. "Inasmuch as ye did it not to one of the least of these, ye did it not to me" (Mt 25:45). To make the identification beyond any doubt, He also puts it positively: "Inasmuch as ye have done it unto one of the least of these my brethren, ye have done it unto me" (Mt 25:40).

This teaching seems to have had a particular appeal for the minds of Christians from the start, giving rise to beautiful legends and treasured incidents. Like St. Christopher whose name is Greek for Christ-bearer. He got his name when he kindly carried an old man on his back across a river, discovering later that the old man was Christ in disguise. Or such as the story of St. Francis who met a repulsive leper who seemed to change into Christ as he looked at him, which enabled the saint to embrace him lovingly.

The purpose behind this kind of identification is that it proves to be a tremendous motivation for acts of kindness and a strong deterrent against malicious deeds. Almost everybody would want to be kind to Christ and would hate to do unpleasant things to Him. Christ hoped that by knowing this truth, we would be eager to do good to all men and be unwilling to hurt them.

We must remember that all those remarks are in the context of the central truth of this chapter, which is that Christ indwells the believer. Consequently, the kind of identification which Jesus speaks of in this verse would have special point to the disciples in their relations with each other. Peter would wince as he remembered, maybe, some incident when he had torn the hide off John for something or other. It meant he had abused His Master, for Christ was within John. Andrew would bite his lips as he recalled, perhaps, a day when he ate more of his share of fish so that James had to be content with a crust of bread. If he had saved it for James, that would have meant giving it to Christ because He was within James.

What a difference this could make to harmony in our churches if this truth were known and acted upon!

When we criticize the Sunday school superintendent, we are taking a slap at God. When we say unkind things about the minister, we are blaming the Father. When we gossip about a fellow Christian, we are blaspheming Christ. When we cause trouble in the church by our selfish egotism, we are sinning against the Holy Spirit.

By the same token Jesus is telling us that if we encourage that Sunday school leader, we are praising God Himself. If we speak words of appreciation to the pastor, we have sung a hymn of love to the Father. If we stop some irresponsible person from maligning our brother, we have shielded Christ's heart from the sword. If we bring harmony to His church, we have made easy the work of the Holy Spirit.

They say that in the Vietnam war, friend and foe dress alike, so a shot may hit a friend as well as an enemy. Likewise Christ wears the same clothes as people. We could crucify Him over again.

The Impact of His Works

The guilt of the persecutors is made all the more certain, Jesus says, because they not only had His heart-piercing words but they witnessed the works which proved He came from God. "If I had not done among them the works which none other man did, they had not had sin: but now have they both seen and hated both me and my Father" (v. 24).

When Jesus brought His new message to the world, people found it devastatingly revolutionary. It challenged the accepted beliefs of centuries. It defied the teachings of the greatest rabbis of His day. To claim that this truth came from God, it had to be substantiated in some way. That witness was the divine vindication that came in His miracles (Jn 5:36). As people watched his ministrations to human suffering and saw healing in impossible cases, they knew that a greater power was with Jesus. When John the Baptist began to doubt whether Jesus was indeed the Messiah, Jesus pointed to these works (Mt 11:2-6).

Some have found the miracles of Jesus hard to believe, and they are if we stop at Jesus of Nazareth. But when we go further and recognize that He was God in Christ (2 Co 5:19), the credibility changes. If God is indeed in our world confronted by human need, we can expect strange things to happen. If they didn't, then we might begin to wonder.

Similar signs followed the ministry of the disciples after Jesus left them (Ac 5:12). They needed vindication even more. Otherwise, who would take notice of a bunch of ignorant peasants?

But we must not assume that miracles occurred every hour in New Testament times. They were even then rare enough to warrant special attention by the Scripture writers. The power to work these miracles was one of the gifts of the Spirit ("charismata," if we wish to get technical). But Paul says that simple benevolent love is a "more excellent way" than them all (1 Co 12:31). Occasionally we have recorded for us written allusions by heathen writers about the early Christians. Yet it isn't the miracles they mention. They probably thought they were tricks anyway. But they stressed the miraculous love of the Christians, not only to each other but to their very persecutors!

Whether the miracles were wonders of nature or victories of

the personality, they told of the presence of God. The Pharisees watched but still turned away. They did not want to be convinced because they did not want to change.

God is still as shadowy to people today as ever, and the Word still needs vindication. We do not see much of nature miracles today. Maybe God doesn't want to appear as a cheap magician, or maybe we aren't expecting enough. In any case, the requirements for belief in divine action are far more subtle. But God still has to be shown in action. Theory or faith is simply not enough.

Jesus has already mentioned answered prayer as a witness (vv. 7-8) and He is as keen on the miracles of love as Paul (v. 13). But there are plenty of possibilities. The curious world outside knows how insoluble some personality problems can be. If they can see victories over evils which hold them powerless, they will recognize the works of God.

Just as the magician on the stage needs volunteers as His guinea pigs, so God does too. He needs people who will have bad enough problems that He will be put to a real test. God still wants to exhibit His works to vindicate His presence.

True, this witness to His power will condemn many because their excuses will be swept away, but they have to have that chance anyway. But besides those who turn away from the Word, there will be many who will be convinced. Neither Christ nor the Father can be seen by human eyes now, but the actions of God in human experience can be readily detected by the spirit of man.

Let's show the world what God can do!

Predestined Unprovoked Hate

The final word of Jesus on how His influence reveals the hidden evil in men, is recorded in verse 25. He is very much aware of how terrifying the thought of unleashed evil can be and therefore now wants to cap it all by a final reminder of what He has talked about before: evil is never unrestrained; it always fulfills the purposes of God in the long run.

This is what He says: "But this cometh to pass, that the

word might be fulfilled that is written in their law, They hated me without a cause."

As it stands, the statement might give the impression that this hate and persecution was brought about by God just to fulfil the Scriptures. But, as we have seen, there is an important distinction that prevents such an error. God only causes evil in the sense that His Word calls for a response which, if denied, will produce evil. Automobile manufacturers cause accidents in the sense that if the drivers do not respond properly disaster will result. But the makers did not intend this. Neither does God.

Since God foresees all this from the beginning of time, He can cause little clues like this to be included in Scripture. The writer may have no idea of all that is involved in it at the time, but the later fulfillment makes it clear. Perhaps to fit in with the context of our thinking, we could paraphrase the passage like this: "What they don't seem to realize is that this bad treatment of me which is their responsibility, is also a fulfillment of something they should have seen in their own law: They hated me without any justification."

Far from implying that the poor Pharisees were caught in the grip of an inexorable fate which caused them to sin, He is saying that their Scriptures, which they professed to know so well, also warned them of the enormity of their offense.

It has been claimed that Jesus is being unfair here. How could the Pharisees possibly know that this obscure reference was to be identified with their present happenings? If Jesus expected them to make such a specific identification, then it would be like saying: "Meet my friend at the airport. You can tell him because he will be wearing a tie."

It makes more sense to assume that Jesus is saying that although hating without justification could be true of countless people, the Pharisees nevertheless should have been well enough aware of the truth of the statement to recognize they were guilty of it. Since the Holy Spirit is the interpreter and enforcer of the Bible, we can be sure that the "two-edged sword" hits its mark all right.

The reference in the statement to "their" law rather than God's law is quite significant. It does not mean that He is denying that the law of the Bible (the allusion is to Psalm 69:4) is indeed God's law. He was always very careful to place on record His respect for that Scripture. He is only trying to emphasize that they were the ones who so proudly felt themselves to be the custodians and experts on the Law. They could not claim ignorance here. They knew, yet they failed to abide by it.

The thrust of what Jesus is saying about the sin itself, is that hating is bad enough at any time but it is at least understandable if someone does some harm to us to warrant the animosity. But when there is no justification for it whatever, it shows just how wicked the heart of the hater is.

It also shows how deep it is. Hatreds that come from isolated acts are often temporary and tend to evaporate quickly, especially if retaliated in kind. The hatreds without justification point to a badly poisoned spirit, and that needs far more radical treatment.

The Pharisees hated Jesus, not because of anything He had done, but because of what He was. His life and message threw light on the hidden corruption in their hearts. They didn't like what they saw, but they couldn't face the remedy either. Therefore they turned on Him, projecting their guilt and anger.

Realistically, this is what we have to expect if our lives are reflecting His. It will be just fine if the people we come in contact with turn from their selfishness and sin and find cleansing. But if they don't, we must expect to be "hated without a cause." It is the occupational hazard of being a disciple.

These verses about the effect of the gospel on the hearts of those who reject Christ are most illuminating about human nature but very sad. As far as self-determination is concerned, we are made like God, even with the power to smash our fist into His face if we wish.

11

The Continuing Life

VERSES 26-27

The Comforter

THERE ARE SOME PEOPLE who let the truth drop where it wills. "If the cap fits, wear it." They feel they have no more responsibility than to proclaim the truth and can disregard whom it hurts. Jesus is not like that. You can detect His tender concern for the disciples as He watches the effect on them of everything He says. At this stage in His message, He is aware that He has been stressing something of the terrible cost of being a disciple, and that they are becoming somewhat fearful. They need something more encouraging now.

Before He talked about this sombre aspect of being a Christian, He had paved the way by stressing that they were not alone because He was with them and in them. But He knows that they are wondering how they are going to get on after He has gone, because He has warned them of this eventuality (Mt 16:21). He is deeply thankful to God that He has made provision through the Comforter. You can readily imagine how the hearts of the disciples lifted when He stated, "But when the Comforter is come . . ." (v. 26). He had already mentioned the Comforter (Jn 14:15), but now He has special relevance.

Let us leave the rest of these inspiring words for a moment and concentrate on that word *comforter*. I know it is perilous exegesis to put too much emphasis on the derivation of Greek words because of the temptation to use this as a device to put meanings into the writer's words which he never intended. But in this instance examining the derivation may be helpful. The Greek word for Comforter, *parakletos,* comes from the root *parakaleo,* which essentially means "I call beyond." It occurs in Romans 12:1 and there is translated "I beseech." The two ideas *comfort* and *beseech* look different, but they have a relationship at their basis.

Let us look at *parakaleo* this way. Someone has called the work of the Paraclete "the supersonic call of God," reminding us of the use of dogs in war time. Because a dog's ears can detect sound waves with a frequency beyond the range of human beings, it was possible to send out signals which could not be detected by the enemy and were drowned out by the noise of battle, yet which could be received by the dogs. They were able to hear that supersonic call and proceed to obey their master's will.

This is a picture to help us understand *parakaleo.* God is calling to us above the clamor of everyday life, because He knows we have a spiritual higher frequency which can detect His call. So in Romans 12:1 the supersonic call is going out to us above the din of our self-centered, frenzied activity, to give our lives in quiet surrender to Him.

When *parakaleo* means to comfort, it refers to those terrible times of heartbreak or bereavement when we are drowned in the noise of our own grief. At those times, when other voices seem empty and meaningless, He reaches our hearts and His voice is like ointment on the hurt of the soul. The disciples are about to face bereavement and heartbreak. God is not only going to speak in comfort, He is going to come in the person of His Holy Spirit. He is not content to send comfort; He is going to come Himself.

What this meant was that God was never going to leave them. He had been with them all this time in the person of His Son and would be revealing Himself soon as God the Spirit. But within their hearts He was the same God. The human Jesus would die on the cross, but the divine Christ would always remain in their hearts. Only their way of looking at things had to change. They had to graduate from reliance upon a physical presence to an unseen spiritual reality.

The big fear of the disciples must have been that their glorious adventure would all end when He left them. Actually, in spite of these words of Jesus, they did assume it was all over when Jesus died. Peter's abandonment of hope was typical. "I go a fishing" (Jn 21:3).

It is just as well for us that it didn't all end with the earthly life of Jesus because then Christianity would have been an episode in history as irrelevant and unreachable by us as the Golden Age of Greece. The Comforter is still here, and Christ in Him abides within the dedicated heart as effectively in the twentieth century as He did in the first.

Sent from the Father

The word *Comforter* in some Bibles is given as "advocate," which does catch some of the significance, too. Of course there are several meanings to advocate in English, but the reference here would be to one who represents God, perhaps such as an attorney who represents his client in dealings with the government or some firm or other person.

This aspect of the meaning of parakletos is underlined by what Jesus says about Him coming from God in this same verse 26. "Whom I will send unto you from the Father . . . which proceedeth from the Father." These apparently innocent words were the basis of one of the most vicious church splits in history, that between the Greek Orthodox church and the Roman Catholic church. The issue was whether the Holy Spirit proceeded from both the Father and the Son or just one of the Persons!

Much of our problem with understanding the Trinity is caused because we try to probe the nature of God. This is about as senseless as a child trying to apprehend quantum mechanics. The being of God belongs to a different medium than our space-time-matter universe. Our medium of space-time-matter is like a vast sphere in which we live. Our minds are tools to deal with what is within space, time, and matter;

but we cannot probe outside it. Yet it is outside where God has His essential being. Consequently, it is only when God shows Himself in our world that we can know Him at all. When we are translated out of this time-matter-space sphere, we can expect minds which will be fashioned to the medium of that other world; and then we will understand. To try now would be useless speculation.

Where we are on solid ground is when God reveals Himself to men in space-time. Consequently our interest is in the manifestations of God. We think of the Father, Son, and Holy Spirit as *ways* in which God works among us. Usage of the word *person* for God does not appear in the Bible at all; when it was used by the early Christians it did not mean an individual such as it does to us now. It meant mask or face, that is, a way of revealing the being wearing it. In the New Testament, Jesus is called God "manifest in the flesh" (1 Ti 3:16).

Now if we were to assume that the persons of God consist only of manifestations of God, we would be going beyond the facts and would be in deep trouble with the theologians. The Bible does imply that in that other world there are distinctions in the persons of the Godhead while God is still one, but we are only concerned with this world. The other can wait.

In this world, the Holy Spirit is God in His executive capacity, carrying out the redeeming work of Christ by trying to win men for Christ and attempting to conserve and continue that work of redemption in the believer. He is sent from God for that purpose. The Holy Spirit then is not some vague impersonal influence. He is God Himself at work.

We have seen earlier that the New Testament does not distinguish much between the Father, Son, and Holy Spirit and often uses the terms synonymously. It never goes into the question of the nature of God's being. In this context we are discussing now, Jesus had an excellent opportunity to comment on the relationship between the Spirit and the Father, but He passed it by. He just was not interested. His only concern was to convince the disciples that their Comforter was from God.

Provided we keep away from previous theological speculation, the work of the Holy Spirit has great relevance to us modern-day disciples. It goes beyond the mere comforting thought that God is still with us. It stresses that He is going to be a working God. The heart where He dwells is going to be a working outfit, not a dude ranch. He is not going to be with us to sit and hold our hands. He is going to lead us into battle.

The Spirit of Truth

The Bible is essentially a book recording the dealings of God with men, so it is a kind of history of the Holy Spirit. It has been aptly remarked that the book of the Acts of the Apostles could have been titled the Acts of the Holy Spirit. This is certainly very true, but so could have been the whole of the Bible. The Holy Spirit is revealed as being incessantly active on behalf of the mankind that God loves so much. I imagine that Jesus would have loved to tell about the Holy Spirit in great detail, but He exercised much more discipline than many of us modern preachers and kept to the point in mind, which was how the Holy Spirit was to comfort the disciples after He had gone.

For this purpose, Jesus confines Himself to just two of the activities of the Holy Spirit—truth and witness. He even refers to the Holy Spirit as the Spirit of Truth. We will look at the witness angle later. On the truth aspect He goes into more detail later. "Howbeit when he, the Spirit of truth, is come, he will guide you into all truth: for he shall not speak of himself; but whatsoever he shall hear, that shall he speak: and he will shew you things to come. He shall glorify me: for he shall receive of mine, and shall shew it unto you." (Jn 16:13-14).

Jesus knew that they would be missing His teaching help especially, because this had been an important element in their friendship from the beginning. As we have seen, most of His truth was not proclaimed to the world at large, but to the disciples.

If we don't understand His obsession with people rather than ideas, this seems a great pity. Think how much richer the world would have been if He had spent those three short precious years of His ministry dictating eternal truths to scribes for posterity! Instead, he patiently taught a group of peasants. Most likely, they promptly forgot almost everything He said, but somehow in the process they were transformed and went out to change the world. How much more wonderful to have a community of people who know God in the intimacy of personal experience than libraries of knowledge about God!

But what was to happen now? The process of their preparation to be the heralds of His message was far from complete. What Jesus says is that they don't have to worry—the Spirit of truth will be with them. They won't be deprived of a thing.

I imagine they still had their doubts. Could this spiritual way of conveying truth be as satisfying as the person-to-person physical contact? Wouldn't it be too subjective? How would they know that it was the Holy Spirit speaking and not just their own thoughts?

These are the same objections that come to us today. The result of leaving things to the Holy Spirit seems to be a mess. The variety of theological opinions among Christians is a sight to behold.

But theology is not the truth He was talking about. Even His own teachings didn't clear up many questions and certainly raised a multitude more. The interest of Jesus is in people and in their redemption, and this does not require infallibility of interpretation. His teaching was directed towards changing people, not just informing them.

In the real essence of things, it doesn't matter so much if John Jones believes in speaking in tongues and Sam Smith doesn't, as long as they use the language of love to each other. The Holy Spirit may not make it clear to them whether they should have fermented wine or grape juice for communion, but He will make it clear that they should drink the nectar of loving fellowship. The Holy Spirit does not seem to be particularly active now in producing oracles of eternal truths. But He is enormously busy telling people how to live the Christian way.

The Holy Spirit's work in giving truth is never mass production. It is always personal and individual. He prescribes according to individual needs. What one Christian gets out of a certain passage of Scripture or out of a sermon may be very different from what another receives. I have even had people receive ideas from my sermons which weren't even there as far as I could see! No doubt they should have been, but that does not stop the Holy Spirit.

When the truth we seek for is the truth of living and not the truths of the absolute, the question whether it is my mind or the Holy Spirit becomes irrelevant. He is in my mind and thinks through my thoughts according to the needs that my heart tells my mind. He abides in me and I abide in Him, so we live together as one divine plus human organism. I don't get any solutions to the inscrutables this way, but I do get the very marrow of satisfying, fulfilled living.

Testifying of Christ

As Jesus sees it, the other great need that the Comforter fills is to be a witness to Himself: "He shall testify of me" (v. 26). This matter of testimony or witness is a most important element in the teachings of Jesus. He agrees firmly with the Old Testament position that unsubstantiated statements have no validity and subjects Himself to the requirement that there must be witnesses to attest the truth of what He says (Jn 5:31). He claims that in His case the main witness is His miraculous works (Jn 5:36).

As we have seen earlier, the disciples faced an impossible task as unlearned country yokels to convince a nation that had more than its share of profound scholars, that God wanted the sacred traditions of the past swept away and replaced by a revolutionary new order. Jesus had His great and mighty works to thunder the conviction that God was behind Him. They needed at least that and more. Jesus realized this, for He once said, speaking of the believer, "Greater works than these shall he do; because I go unto my Father" (Jn 14:12). Now He is implying that the Comforter will enable them to accomplish this. This seems to be why, before He left them, He urged them to wait for the Pentecost experience before they started on their task of evangelizing the world.

These signs were forthcoming. Things like the sudden ability to speak foreign languages staggered the crowd at Pentecost, and the healing of the cripple at the Gate Beautiful turned the city on its ear. There could be no doubt that a power greater than these simple men was at work. The message was attested and thousands believed. This kind of testimony has been discussed in detail earlier.

However, this does not appear to be all that Jesus meant by the witness of the Spirit. There is also a mystic way in which the Comforter testifies to Christ similar to what has been referred to in the last section. When the message is preached, it comes from the lips of mere men and therefore may be true or false or, more often, a mixture of both. The Holy Spirit is present on those occasions and makes His own impact on the mind of the hearer so that he may become convinced the message is true.

It is important to qualify this by the inclusion of that word "may," for whether a man is convinced or not is far more than an intellectual matter. It depends on the response of the will.

When a person first hears the claims of Christ, his natural reaction is to doubt and this is as it should be. If we promptly believed everything we heard in the name of religion, we certainly would be in a mess. Doubt is to the mind what pain is to the body, an indication of danger.

This kind of doubt which appraises a message to determine its truth is not at all reprehensible. It must be clearly distinguished from the unbelief which Jesus so vigorously condemns (e.g., Jn 8:24). Unbelief in the New Testament sense is a refusal to open the mind to truth because of an unwillingness to commit the life to Christ anyway. This kind of person cannot be convinced regardless of the evidence.

It is to the honest doubter that the Holy Spirit turns, to the one who has too much moral integrity to believe without sufficient evidence, but who is wide open to accept the truth if the facts are there. This does not mean that the Holy Spirit is some kind of star debater, heaping fact upon fact, or involving Himself in a complicated chain of agreement. He will not try to explain all the mysteries of Christ, but He will seek to convince us that the truth is reasonable. This also was His policy in the Old Testament (Is 1:18). By its very nature, divine truth has to be *beyond* reason, but it cannot be *against* reason.

The prime thrust of the Holy Spirit will be to the heart and not to the head. This does not mean an appeal to the emotions but rather to experience. The seeker must sense that the message is true. This is not as unscientific as it seems, because scientific truth is usually first discovered that way. The scientist gets a flash of insight that a heart could be transplanted, that a hovercraft principle would work, that a laser could transmit messages. Personally, I think this is a work of the Holy Spirit, too, because with Him there is no difference between secular and sacred.

Of course, after sensing the truth the scientist has the laborious task of proving it. When the spiritual pilgrim senses the truth of the message of Christ and commits himself as a result, he has to prove it too, in the laboratory of experience.

The testimony of the Holy Spirit to Christ never ceases. No person can ever claim that he couldn't believe because of insufficient evidence. Wherever there is an honest, earnest seeking heart, the Comforter is never far away.

The Witness of the Disciples

The final word of Jesus in this chapter is still on the theme of His continuing life through the Comforter, only now He wants to stress the part of the disciples in the work of the Holy Spirit. He says, "And ye also shall bear witness, because ye have been with me from the beginning" (v. 27). They are not merely to be comforted in His absence. They are with the Comforter, to help fill the gap caused by His leaving.

If they had known how things would turn out, they would have been staggered at just how powerful their witness was to become. Not only would they continue His life and message, but they were destined to magnify it a thousand times. It is just as well that they didn't know that their new faith would be locked in a terrible struggle with the might of Rome. Even if they had known, they never would have believed that three centuries hence, the Roman emperor would bow the knee to the Christ of whom they witnessed.

The witness of the disciples to Christ took two main forms: spreading the Gospel and making the New Testament Scriptures. In a later message Jesus too stressed that their evangelism was to be by way of witness in cooperating with the Holy Spirit. "But ye shall receive power, after that the Holy Ghost is come upon you: and ye shall be witnesses unto me" (Ac 1:8).

They considered it was their job to testify of all that Jesus did and taught, and what happened to Him. Their gospel was very simple and was quite uncluttered with theological requirements, just the proclamation of the death, burial, and resurrection of Christ (1 Co 15:1-5), which were events that they had personally seen and to the truth of which they could testify.

But after such a message as this about their spiritual union with Christ, it would be clear to them that their testimony could not stop at the events of the earthly life of Jesus. He had a continuing life in them, and they must witness to the miracles of that life.

Earlier in this book it has been mentioned that the way Jesus puts this matter of witnessing is significant. He does not expressly tell them to witness. He says they are to *be* witnesses. They are to let the miracle of the life of Christ work through them that people can see through to the Christ within.

This is what happened. If the records in the book of Acts are any indication, their spoken messages were not anything to write home about. But oh, the impact of their transformed lives! The smashing success of their efforts was not so much an explosion but an implosion. People were drawn in to Christ by what they saw happening.

Their other great achievement in witness was the New Testament, and this followed the same lines as their spoken testimony. The gospels described and testified to the earthly life of

Jesus. The epistles were concerned with the continuing life of Jesus within the soul. The Bible is a work of the Holy Spirit yet also a human testimony. As they wrote, they searched their hearts and minds to recall their experiences with Jesus, so it came out with all the color and warmth of their personalities, yet watched over by the Comforter so that it would fit His plans and suit the needs of all people.

Because of the witness to Christ, which is the New Testament, we are far better equipped to carry out our responsibilities as witnesses than they were. We can measure what we think and feel and do by that sure Word of God. We also have the treasure of church history; two thousand years of personal experiential witness to what Christ can do.

Yet, strange to say, without us all this would have little impact. It is not just that we are needed to tell people what God has wrought in the past. We could cross a robot with a tape recorder to do that. Each age has to see its own people experiencing. Even the most impressive instances in the past do not seem to hit the spot. They have to see Christianity work in us.

Thus the message of Jesus in John 15 goes full circle. It starts off by showing how necessary it is for us to be as a branch abiding in the vine, so that His life flows through ours. It finishes by throwing us back on the same resource because the witness to others has no substance without it.

"Arise, let us go hence" (Jn 14:31).

Questions for Study and Discussion

CHAPTER 1

1. In view of the message of John 15, are our evangelistic messages adequate?
2. How much of the work of God in the soul is automatic?
3. Does God have fixed prerequisites for salvation which apply in every case including, for example, children and mental deficients?
4. Were people who subsequently abandoned their Christian profession really converted in the first place?
5. How can we convince a scientific world that God exists?

CHAPTER 2

1. To what extent should we "leave things to the Lord"?
2. If a child is killed by a drunken driver's negligence, can we still say that the Lord took the child?
3. How can I tell whether God is guiding me to a particular job that I am offered?
4. How rapid can we expect our progress in fruitfulness to be?
5. How does God the Gardener deal with a nation?

CHAPTER 3

1. Some of the early church Fathers felt that noble Greeks, such as Socrates, who lived before Christ, were Christians. Could this be true?
2. Could Jesus have accidentally cut a table leg too short?
3. In what sense is the Bible infallible?

4. Should we shift churches if our minister is a poor preacher?
5. To what extent is conscience the voice of God?

Chapter 4

1. Does an active Christian have to be "religious"?
2. Studdert Kennedy, a great World War I chaplain, committed suicide because of depression due to the sufferings he saw. Was this in any sense Christian?
3. How can we evangelize by shared action?
4. What is the source of Christian unhappiness?
5. How can we abide in Christ in our town?

Chapter 5

1. In view of the fact that Jesus says, "without me ye can do nothing," how were our great Jewish citizens able to do so much?
2. Should we pray for the weather we need?
3. Why does it seem that people are losing confidence in the church?
4. What was Jesus teaching through the story of the importunate widow?
5. What is involved in modern discipleship?

Chapter 6

1. In view of what Jesus says about love, how do we explain gossip and criticism among Christians?
2. What should we do when we find we can't conquer a resentment?
3. Is tithing necessarily Christian?
4. How happy can we realistically expect a Christian under trial to be?
5. Comment on this statement: "The world is not interested in how good we are but how happy we are."

Chapter 7

1. In view of what Jesus says about friendship, why is it so hard to get Christian workers?

2. How can we explain the variety of beliefs among Christians?
3. What part has feeling or emotion in friendship with Christ?
4. Is this friendship sufficient to conquer human loneliness?
5. Why do you think Abraham was called the friend of God?

Chapter 8

1. Predestination carried too far destroys moral responsibility. Explain.
2. Is the clergy as a separate class justified in our modern world?
3. "There is nothing so perilous as ignorance in action": comment on this statement in view of the truths of this chapter.
4. Why do the Scriptures say Jesus has to be called Emmanuel (Mt 1:23) when He never used that name?
5. Does it make any difference which person of the Trinity we pray to?

Chapter 9

1. How popular can a Christian be?
2. Many Christians in Russia avoid persecution by keeping out of politics. Is this right?
3. Are any amusements necessarily worldly?
4. In view of Christ's apparent lack of success, how much can we expect in Christian work?
5. What is the cross that Christians have to bear today?

Chapter 10

1. Why is it that a minister often gets more opposition from his members than from the world?
2. How will God deal with children who die in infancy and who could not, therefore, exercise faith?
3. What does God do with the heathen who never hear the gospel?
4. Is it possible for a Jew to love God sincerely and yet not be able honestly to accept Jesus as His Son?

5. What is the difference between being hated without a cause and being hated without a reason?

CHAPTER 11

1. Comment on the statement, "To understand the Trinity or the nature of God we would have to be God ourselves."
2. What is meant by saying that the Holy Spirit is the executor of the Godhead?
3. What can we expect today when we are filled with the Spirit?
4. Why (apparently) did Jesus never speak in tongues?
5. Can we be adequate witnesses without spoken witnessing?